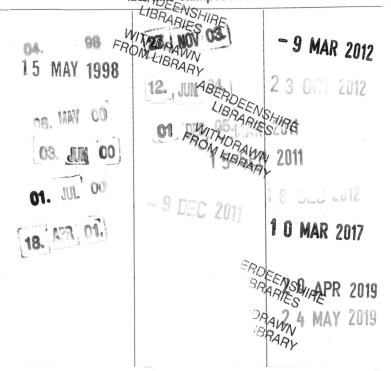

Royal
Commission on the
Ancient and
Historical
Monuments of
Scotland

Aberdeen on Record

IMAGES OF THE PAST

Photographs and Drawings of the

National Monuments Record of Scotland

Edinburgh: The Stationery Office

Published by The Stationery Office and
available from:

The Stationery Office Bookshops
71 Lothian Road, Edinburgh EH3 9AZ
(counter service only)
59-60 Holborn Viaduct, London EC1A 2FD
(temporary location, fax orders only)
Fax 0171-831 1326
68-69 Bull Street, Birmingham B4 6AD
0121-236 9696 Fax 0121-236 9699
33 Wine Street, Bristol BS1 2BQ
0117-926 4306 Fax 0117-929 4515
9-21 Princess Street, Manchester M60 8AS
0161-834 7201 Fax 0161-833 0634
16 Arthur Street, Belfast BT1 4GD
01232 238451 Fax 01232 235401
The Stationery Office Oriel Bookshop
The Friary, Cardiff CF1 4AA
01222 395548 Fax 01222 384347

**The Stationery Office publications are also
available from:**

The Publications Centre
(mail, telephone and fax orders only)
PO Box 276, London SW8 5DT
General enquiries 0171-873 0011
Telephone orders 0171-873 9090
Fax orders 0171-873 8200

Accredited Agents
(see Yellow Pages)

and through good booksellers

First published 1997 by The Stationery Office Limited,
South Gyle Crescent, Edinburgh EH12 9EB

Applications for reproduction should be made to the Crown
Copyright Unit, St Clements House, 2–16 Colegate, Norwich NR3
1BQ

British Library Cataloguing in Publication Data

A catalogue record of this book is available from the British Library

ISBN 0 11 495818 1

Designed by Jim Cairns

AE
1043831

Contents

Introduction

This volume brings together a selection of photographs and drawings relating to the buildings and archaeological sites of the City of Aberdeen, drawn chiefly from the collections of the National Monuments Record of Scotland (NMRS). These illustrations show the diversity of the NMRS collections, which embrace photographs and drawings of various dates, together with an extensive library of books and pamphlets. They also demonstrate the extent of NMRS coverage of one of our country's great cities, including its everyday building-types as well as its architectural set-pieces. The greatest emphasis falls naturally on the period of incessant transformation and modernisation in the 19th and 20th centuries, but there is also a wealth of material on earlier periods. The volume also includes a summary of the various extant collections of visual records of the Aberdeen built environment (many publicly accessible), both in the NMRS and elsewhere – including the rich collections within the city itself.

The Royal Commission on the Ancient and Historical Monuments of Scotland (RCAHMS) was founded in 1908 as a national agency for the recording of the built heritage, a task which, for the first half-century of its existence, it mainly carried out through the compilation and publication of county-by-county *Inventories*. From 1966 the emphasis gradually shifted to the enhancement of the Royal Commission's archive, the National Monuments Record of Scotland, through the collection of existing material (such as architects' plans) and by making new records of important buildings and industrial sites, especially those under threat of demolition or significant alteration. One of the main elements in this recording work is the Topographical Survey, an area-by-area photographic survey of the country, which perpetuates the systematic geographical approach of the *Inventories*, but in a more rapid and flexible form (including provision for total oblique aerial coverage of selected urban areas). The City of Aberdeen was surveyed in this way in 1991–2. All of the activities mentioned above – architectural, archaeological and industrial – are reflected in the contents of this book.

The text was written by Miles Glendinning (who also acted as editor), Graham Ritchie and Jane Thomas; Lesley Ferguson supplied the archaeological entries in Part 2. Photographic work was undertaken by the staff of the Photographic Department; graphic work was undertaken by the staff of the Drawing Office (in both cases including some previous survey work). We would like to thank the following for reading through and (where applicable) commenting on drafts of the text: Ian Beavan; Bill Brogden; Alison Brown; Judith Cripps; Mike Dey; Elma Garden; Iain Gray; Neil Lamb; George Massie; Murray Pittock; W. F. Ritchie; Ian Shepherd; Anne and Grant Simpson; and Judith Stones. For other assistance, grateful thanks are due to the following: Jenny, Ben, Sophie, Phoebe and Clara Benjamin; Colin and Molly Morrison; David Murray Associates; Dr Pat Torrie.

Copyright and reproduction rights held by organisations or individuals are indicated in the captions to the illustrations. All other illustrations are Crown Copyright, RCAHMS. Reference numbers to illustrations forming part of the NMRS collections are included at the end of the captions. Copies of these illustrations may be purchased by writing to: The Secretary, RCAHMS, John Sinclair House, 16 Bernard Terrace, Edinburgh EH8 9NX (quoting the reference numbers listed in the captions).

MAPS   Sections from Ordnance Survey map
LXXV, first edition 1869 and (opposite) second
edition, 1902.

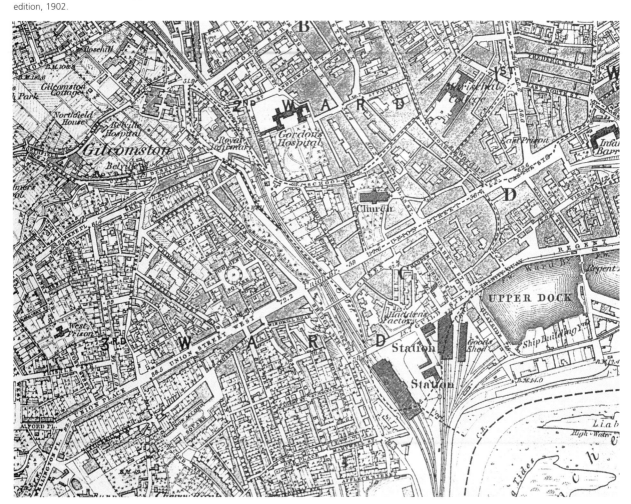

PART 1

Historical and Archaeological Overview

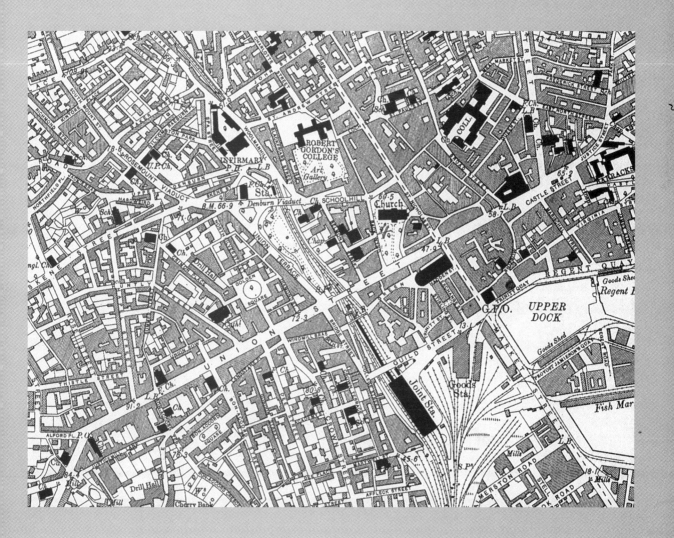

1   Aberdeen around 1300 AD: this reconstruction of life in the medieval backyards is based on archaeological evidence derived from excavations at 42 St Paul Street and drawn by Gavin Smith. The original is in Provost Skene's House (City of Aberdeen Art Gallery and Museums Collections).

2   Excavation in progress, 42 St Paul Street, one of several productive sites excavated prior to the construction of the Bon Accord and St Nicholas shopping centres (Aberdeen Excavation Archive, in RCAHMS E6 34 9).

CHAPTER 1

Archaeological Introduction

3 Section of well-preserved wattle fencing at 42 St Paul Street. Aberdeen excavations have proved particularly rich in organic remains, including wood, leather and textiles (Aberdeen Excavation Archive, in RCAHMS E6 29).

4 Oval storage pit associated with a late medieval stone building at 42 St Paul Street (Aberdeen Excavation Archive, in RCAHMS E6 34 13).

The growth of the City of Aberdeen owes much to its geographical location. The great rivers of the Dee and the Don flow into the North Sea within 4 km of one another and offer natural routes of communication from the coast to the resources of Deeside and Donside. To the south, the eastern knuckle of the Grampians constricts communication except along the tops of the coastal cliffs. It is thus no surprise to find evidence of settlement from the earliest times around what was to become Aberdeen. The aerial view of the city today (see Frontispiece) clearly shows the rivers themselves, the crook in the Don that was to be part of the story of the earliest Christian activity and the great docks at the mouth of the Dee. The coastal zone with the groynes of the beach and the grass-covered sand dunes behind is clearly visible, and Pittodrie Stadium stands out as a recognisable component of the eastern fringe of the modern city.

Inland from the strip of dunes, a ridge of sands and gravels of glacial origin runs north and south between the Dee and the Don, and there appears to have been an area of marsh and lochans to the west. It is hardly surprising that early settlement was concentrated on the better drained land provided by the ridge, which was bisected by what is now called the Powis Burn, with Old Aberdeen spreading southwards from St Machar's and Aberdeen expanding northwards from the administrative centre of the castle and the church of St Nicholas. The pattern is clearly shown on Parson Gordon of Rothiemay's map of 1661; this was the basis for the evocative model, now in Provost Skene's House, which clearly shows the topography of the growing town of the mid-17th century (see also Figure 21). Excavations in Aberdeen have uncovered remarkable evidence of the buildings and associated pottery, bone and stone artefacts of the earlier medieval period, as well as organic remains (see Figures 1–4).

Archaeological evidence indicates that the earliest occupation of the area followed the end of the last glaciation with the arrival of people for whom the resources of the shore, the rivers and the forests offered the staples of life and shelter. Several examples of the tiny flint tools that are characteristic of this hunter-forager way of life have been found throughout the area, but the most important excavations have taken place at Nether Mills of Crathes on Deeside and at Birkwood, near Banchory. On the Green, near the mouth of the Denburn in Aberdeen itself, excavations have uncovered a flint-working floor where flint nodules were fashioned into scrapers and boring tools as well as tiny edge-tools that could be mounted to form fishing spears, or throwing- or cutting-implements. It is difficult to date such meagre evidence, but it is likely that small groups of hunting and gathering peoples had made their way into the

5   Tyrebagger Recumbent Stone Circle drawn by Fred R. Coles, National Museum of Antiquities of Scotland, in the course of his survey of the stone circles of parts of Aberdeenshire and Kincardineshire in 1899 (RCAHMS C77564).

6   The Lang Stane, Hilton, was photographed in a rural setting in 1906 by James Ritchie, a schoolmaster at Port Elphinstone, whose photographs of many archaeological sites in the north-east make an important contribution to the recording of antiquities (AB/2490).

catchments of the Dee, Don and Ythan by 7000 BC. By the beginning of the fourth millennium BC a way of life that depended on agriculture and stock-rearing was being introduced into northern Scotland, but there is little specific archaeological evidence within the city itself. However, at Balbridie, on Deeside, excavation has revealed a large timber structure, which was the home of a community of farmers, growing different wheats and barleys, and using well-fired round-based pottery. A necessary tool for forest clearance and timber construction was the stone axehead, which, when set into a wooden haft, makes an effective implement. Such axeheads might be exchanged over long distances, and examples that have originated in Antrim are known from the north-east, but local sources of hard rock were also used. The burial places of such farming communities are marked by distinctive long mounds of stone or earth, which are often situated in a location that helps to emphasise their size. The building of such mounds represented considerable physical effort by the community. One such mound survives, albeit in a denuded state, at Longcairn on the western edge of the city, measuring about 49 m in length and up to 16 m in breadth.

The stone circles of the north-east caught the imagination of early antiquaries and they are among the most fully recorded monuments. Many of the upright stones are impressive in themselves, but the recumbent stone circles of the region are especially remarkable feats of construction. The principal component comprises a massive stone laid on its side rather than on end with the two tallest stones of the circle as flankers on either side usually situated on the south-western side of the circle; the other stones decrease in size so that the smallest stones are opposite the recumbent one. The circles are difficult to date, but construction within the late third millennium BC is likely, though their use probably extends into the second millennium BC, for their frequently prominent positions would have ensured that they remained potent ritual locations. The best-preserved of the stone circles in Aberdeen itself is that on Tyrebagger Hill, overlooking Dyce Airport, where the recumbent is a massive granite slab weighing some 24 tons, and the flanking uprights are particularly impressive (see Figure 5). A circle that has been disturbed over the passage of time remains at Binghill, while a substantial triangular monolith at Mundurno may be all that survives of another. Single standing stones are sometimes interpreted as territorial- or route-markers or may relate to burial sites; the Gouk Stone and the Lang Stane, Hilton, remain in position (see Figure 6). A remarkable, though more recent, series of upright stones continues the tradition; these are the March Stones indicating the boundary of the Freedom Lands, including Stocket Forest granted to Aberdeen by King Robert the Bruce in 1319, the numbered stones being set into position between 1790 and 1810, and several replacing large boulders with a single

7 Cist at Scotstoun, Bridge of Don, excavated by I. B. M. Ralston in advance of house construction in 1975. The cist had clay-luted corners and a pebble floor, and contained a crouched inhumation with a complete pottery Beaker and two flint artefacts (I. B. M. Ralston/Historic Scotland).The recording of cists and their contents has resulted in a fine anatomical and ceramic collection in Marischal College Museum.

cup-like depression. A boulder with prehistoric cup-and-ring markings may still be seen at Blacktop, a form of decoration that has for long puzzled antiquarians.

One of the most frequent archaeological discoveries in Aberdeenshire is that of a cist-burial, a rectangular coffin of four upright slabs and a capstone set into the ground to receive a crouched inhumation and often accompanied by a pottery vessel of a type known as a Beaker (see Figure 7). The recording of such information, often at short notice as a result of agricultural or building activities, has fallen to successive generations of museum curators and now to Council archaeologists, and an important body of evidence has been gathered about burial practices in the later third and earlier second millennia BC. Several round cairns, with traditional names such as Cat Cairn and Baron's Cairn, dating broadly to the early second millennium BC, can be seen on Tullos Hill. At West Cults, a well-preserved cairn, measuring some 20 m in diameter and 5 m in height, has provided a name for the adjacent Cairn Road; at the Slacks in Kirkhill Forest there is a fine round cairn some 21 m in diameter and 2.5 m high.

The evidence for structures relating to settlement in the second and first millennia BC is lacking, but from discoveries in other parts of the area substantial timber houses may be assumed. By the early centuries AD the inhabitants of the north-east were known to the Romans as the Taexali, though it is not recorded what they called themselves, and they presumably spoke a form of Celtic.

The passage of Roman arms in the north has left a pattern of temporary camps, earthworks comprising a bank and ditch that surrounded the tented camps of an army on the move. Agricola's campaign against the Caledonian tribes is indicated by a series of temporary camps from Raedykes to the south of the Mounth, *via* Normandykes in Peterculter, to Kintore, Durno, Ythan Wells, Auchinhove, Muiryfold and Bellie on the Moray coast. It has been suggested that the battle of Mons Graupius in AD 83 may have taken place on the slopes of Bennachie to the south west of Durno, where aerial photographs show the outline of the largest temporary camp to the north of the Forth, suggesting a considerable concentration of forces. Part of the perimeter ditch and rampart of the temporary camp at Normandykes can still be seen on the ground, the ditch some 4 m in width and the rampart still 2 m high, but for the most part it can only be seen as cropmarkings on aerial photographs (see Figure 8). It is quite likely that harbour facilities at the mouth of the

8   Normandykes, Roman Temporary Camp: the corner of the earthwork shows as a cropmark on an aerial photograph (RCAHMS AB/4544).

9   Two of the Pictish stones at Dyce, photographed by James Ritchie in 1903 (RCAHMS AB/5340)

10   Early Christian cross-slab from Seaton, formerly built into a wall in Don Street, Aberdeen, now in St Machar's Cathedral, photographed by James Ritchie (RCAHMS A8650).

Dee were used by the Roman fleet; certainly the Roman names for the rivers Dee and Don are known – Deva and Devona – the earliest names in the area to be recorded. Although several Roman coins have been found in Aberdeen, they need not be contemporary losses.

By the end of the third century the peoples of the north were known to the Romans as the Picti, or Painted People, but the new name does not imply any movement of population. The Picts have left many distinctively decorated carved slabs; the earliest bear motifs whose meaning is now lost, but later examples also include a cross, a juxtaposition that demonstrates that the symbolism did not conflict with a Christian message. A group of stones at Dyce suggests the presence of an important centre in the area (see Figure 9). One of several traditions has it that Christianity was brought to Aberdeen by St Machar, a follower of St Columba, who was instructed to find a bend in a river in the shape of a crook and to build a church there. One early Christian cross, formerly built into a wall on Don Street, now has a more appropriate location in St Machar's Cathedral (see Figure 10).

CHAPTER 2

Middle Ages and Renaissance

As hinted above, the story of medieval and renaissance Aberdeen is in fact the story of two settlements: the royal burgh of Aberdeen (or 'New' Aberdeen), which grew up around a natural harbour at the mouth of the River Dee, and the episcopal burgh of (Kirktoun of) Aberdon, subsequently known as 'Old Aberdeen', which grew up around St Machar's Cathedral and King's College. The two settlements, although near one another, were physically distinct and surrounded by their croft territories. Even by the late Middle Ages, however, 'New' Aberdeen had become one of the four wealthiest burghs in Scotland; during the 19th and early 20th centuries the city grew to such an extent that Old Aberdeen was swallowed up within its boundaries. In this chapter only, the two towns will be separately discussed.

The Royal Burgh of Aberdeen (New Aberdeen)

Already a royal burgh at the time of the earliest surviving royal charter (by King William the Lion in about 1179), Aberdeen was an unwalled trading community, whose economy was based on fishing and processing of animal products such as wool and leather, and the manufacture of goods from them. By comparison with many other burghs, Aberdeen has always been tied especially closely to its hinterland. Burgh status conferred local economic privileges, including revenues and toll exemptions. The social structure of the burgh was dominated by the burgesses, who were mostly rich merchants, together with an élite group of craftsmen. The tradesmen, by the 15th century, were already formed into Incorporated Trades. By the early 15th century, the population was perhaps around 4,000, and by the early 17th century it had grown to between 7,500 and 10,000.

The plan of the burgh was roughly cruciform. There is uncertainty as to the location of the burgh's first nucleus, but by the end of the Middle Ages the principal street, and market-place, was the east-west Castlegate; this was first mentioned *c.*1290 and referred to as a *'forum'* by Robert III (see Figure 11). It was intersected by the main north-south route linking Old Aberdeen to the harbour (*via* the Gallowgate and Broadgate to the north of Castlegate, and Shiprow on the south). Narrow streets at the west end of Castlegate, running around St Katherine's Hill, gave access to the harbour and to the area known as the Green (possibly the location of the burgh's first settlement, and an early market-place). The tidal harbour, or Gawpuyl, was guarded at the harbour-mouth by a blockhouse (built 1513–42). In response to growing European trade, improvements began in 1608–18 with the removal of an obstructive rock, 'Craig Metallan', by

11   Aerial view (1989) of the medieval core of Aberdeen from the south, showing the redevelopments and new streets of the 19th and 20th centuries. The Town House (tolbooth) is at the extreme centre right and St Nicholas's Church at centre left. (RCAHMS B22553).

David Anderson of Finzeauch, but the harbour still remained shallow and unpredictable. Situated along a beach to the east of the burgh was the small linear fishing settlement of Futty (later Footdee). Also located at some distance, and still standing today, is the old Bridge of Dee, one of the country's oldest surviving stone bridges – a seven-arched structure built from 1518 under Bishop Dunbar. It originally gave land traffic access to the south, just as the tall, pointed Brig o' Balgownie near Old Aberdeen (conceived under Bishop Elphinstone) gave access to the north.

The burgh was dominated by the principal monuments of temporal and ecclesiastical power: Castlegate, for example, was flanked at its east end by the castle, which existed by 1264, but was destroyed by warfare before the reign of David II, and at its west end (beyond the Netherkirkgate) by St Nicholas's Parish Church, first mentioned in 1157. St Nicholas's was the earliest large church in Scotland known to have been aisled – a telling indication of the status of the burgh at that stage – and retains important

12   Photograph (1972) of late 12th-century north transept (Collison's Aisle) of St Nicholas's Church, with Gibbs's West Church to the right and Simpson's restored East Church to the left (RCAHMS AB/3329).

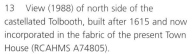

13   View (1988) of north side of the castellated Tolbooth, built after 1615 and now incorporated in the fabric of the present Town House (RCAHMS A74805).

evidence of Transitional architecture in its crossing. The original structure of the church, which later came to include the stone-vaulted St Mary's Chapel of *c*.1438, Aberdeen's only all-granite medieval building, was completed in 1508 with the building of the choir. Stripped of its altars and divided in two at the Reformation, the West Church was rebuilt by James Gibbs in 1751–5, while the East Church was demolished and rebuilt in 1835 (see Figure 12, as well as Figures 23 and 122). The pre-Reformation burgh was dotted with numerous other ecclesiastical buildings, standing out through their stone construction; these included 13th-century Dominican, Carmelite and Trinitarian friaries and a Franciscan house of *c*.1469. A leper hospital (first mentioned in 1363, but in ruins by 1661) was located outside the burgh on Spital Hill; and other hospitals for the sick, built from the late 12th century onwards. The Reformation did not bring these initiatives to an end. In 1593 George Keith, 4th Earl Marischal, founded a new college, Marischal College, in the burgh (based on the lands and rents of the Franciscans) to teach a reformed curriculum in rivalry to the clerical-dominated King's College. Oligarchic control of burgh affairs continued after the Reformation, now by the Town Council and Kirk Session.

The burgh's principal surviving civic monument was added in the early 17th century: the rebuilt Tolbooth. Following the collapse of the steeple of the old, 15th-century tolbooth in 1589, Thomas Watson, a mason from Old Rayne, was contracted after 1615 to construct a new tolbooth, to be 'bigget fyve woult hicht with ane stepill, with ane passage to the knock and batteling be itselff'.[1] As built, it was a massive tower with bartizans. The steeple, with spire, was eventually added in 1629 (see Figure 13).

Among domestic buildings, most were timber-framed, wattle-and-daub walled houses, with thatched roofs, laid out on long, thin 'burgage plots'. The houses were often separated from the street by drystone walled forelands and tradesmen's wooden forebooths; the backlands to the rear were mostly used for cottage industry or gardens. By the late Middle Ages, gradually increasing densities resulted in the building of houses in the backlands or at right angles to the street. By 1317 at least one stone house existed in Gallowgate, but until the beginning of the 16th century, stone houses remained rare. Subsequently, especially in wealthy streets such as Castlegate, Gallowgate and Exchequer Row, but also outside the burgh boundaries, stone houses of the landed classes or rich burgesses began to rise; until the 1740s most houses of this standing were of imported freestone, not granite. Some were like miniature versions of castellated country houses: for example, the original L-plan tower of Provost Skene's House (1545; expanded to its present size in the 17th

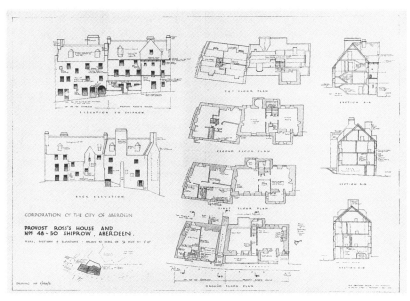

14   Drawings done in 1952 by the City Architect's Department of Provost Ross's House prior to restoration (RCAHMS C21178).

15   View (1992) of Provost Skene's House (built 1545 and expanded in the 17th century) following its rebuilding and incorporation into the open-planned Modernist civic grouping of St Nicholas House (built from 1965) (RCAHMS B55371).

century, with notable cycle of ceiling paintings) or the Z-plan Keith of Benholm Lodging, probably built 1610–16 (and moved in the 1960s to Tillydrone) (see Figure 15, and also Figures 103, 118 and 119). Others, such as 64 Shiprow (1692) were more urban in character, with ground floor shops and upper floor dwellings (See Figure 14, and also Figures 118, 120 and 124). Another noted castellated dwelling, ornamented with bartizans, was 'Jamesone's House', Schoolhill, built in 1586 by Andro Jamesone (now demolished). His son, the painter, George Jamesone, in 1635 founded the town's first park, the semi-public 'Four Nukit Gardyn' (at Woolmanhill). Speaking probably of these houses of the rich, Parson James Gordon of Rothiemay in 1661 described dwellings 'of stone and lyme, rigged above, covered with slaits, mostly of thrie or four stories hight, some of them higher'.[2]

Old Aberdeen

Following the establishment of a bishopric in 1125–30, the first cathedral was possibly begun in the 12th century. A larger replacement was built during the episcopate of Henry Cheyne (1282–1328) and enlarged by Bishop Alexander Kinninmund (1355–80). Its nave was completed in 1422–40 by Bishop Henry Lichton's severe granite west front, with its flanking tower-house-like pavilions and central row of seven lights. A central steeple was begun by Bishop Elphinstone, and western spires (along with a richly painted heraldic nave ceiling) by his successor, Gavin Dunbar (bishop 1518–32). The choir of the cathedral, in its final form, was seemingly never completed, and remains in a ruinous, 14th-century state. Stylistically, the cathedral was Late Gothic, with some elements of neo-Romanesque – a combination common in later medieval Scottish architecture, but nowhere else carried through with such idiosyncratic power (see Figures 16 and 17, and also Figures 123 and 126). Following the Reformation, St Machar's gradually fell into decay; there were attacks by Protestant extremists, and following the demolition of the choir by an English army in the 1650s, the central steeple collapsed in 1688. The 17th century also saw the reduction to ruins of St Maria ad Nives (Snow) Church, built c.1503 by Bishop Elphinstone as a separate parish church for Old Aberdeen.

16   Drawing done in 1883 by Alexander McGibbon of the west front of St Machar's Cathedral (RCAHMS ABD/42/12).

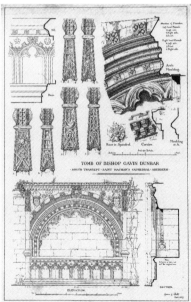

17   Drawing done in 1885 by James Watt of tomb of Bishop Gavin Dunbar, St Machar's Cathedral (RCAHMS C21183).

18   View (1991) of main west front of King's College, showing the chapel and crown steeple, and additions of 1825–32 by John Smith (RCAHMS B57217).

The settlement of Kirktoun of Aberdon had become a burgh of barony in 1489; the bishop was baron until c.1597, and council proceedings are on record from 1602. By then, the second main element of the burgh had been established: Bishop Elphinstone's King's College, founded in 1495 under the aegis of King James IV to teach a classical humanist curriculum modelled on that of Paris. The original college group, built from c.1498–1505, was quadrangular on plan, and topped by a crown steeple (rebuilt 1633 after destruction by a storm). It was known to have been built on swampy ground, using timber foundations (see Figure 18, and also Figure 100).

The original burgh was contained within an approximate rectangle bounded by the Chanonry and Don Street, but in its developed form at the beginning of the 17th century the burgh had assumed an elongated, north-south layout along a well-trafficked (but, until 1636, unpaved) route stretching south from Brig o' Balgownie (built c.1320) to the northern outskirts of Aberdeen. The population of 900 mainly comprised artisans, linked to craft guilds, and their families, as well as a handful of lairds.

The original core of the burgh, consisting of the Chanonry, was bounded by four ports or gates, and before the Reformation contained the manses and quarters of the ecclesiastical dignitaries, built of stone and slated. Two of the most significant of these – the now-demolished episcopal palace, and Chaplains' Court – imitated the quadrangular courtyard plans of the royal palaces, with a tower at each corner. Chaplains' Court was built in 1519 by Bishop Dunbar; one side of it, including one of the towers, survives today, having been incorporated in an 18th-century enlargement (see also Figure 116). South of the Chanonry lay the main part of the burgh, around the High Street, with its burgage-plot layout and thatched houses, rather like those of Aberdeen. South of the High Street stretched the academic precinct of the burgh, dominated by King's College; post-Reformation additions to the latter included the tenement-like 'Cromwell Tower' of students' lodgings built in 1658 (see Figures 19 and 20).

19   View of Old Aberdeen from the south, from John Slezer's *Theatrum Scotiae* (c. 1693), the first Scottish topographical book to provide bird's-eye views of principal burghs, houses and gardens. St Machar's Cathedral, with central tower, is in the middle of the view, and King's College to the right (RCAHMS ABD/50/23).

20   Aerial view (1989) of Old Aberdeen, with High Street running diagonally across: King's College is at bottom right and the postwar buildings, laid out to a master-plan by Robert Matthew (1957), are at upper left (RCAHMS B22243).

Conclusion

The period is demarcated sharply from the next phase of Aberdeen's development, after 1660. The outbreak of civil war in 1639 was followed by successive invasions and occupations, culminating in the sacking of the town by Montrose's troops in September 1644; General Monck's English army entered the town in 1651 and built a fort on Castlehill, using material from the ruins of St Machar's Cathedral. Some 10 per cent of the population died in the conflicts of the 1640s, and 25 per cent in the plague of 1647.

CHAPTER 3

Rothiemay to Abercrombie

1660–1800

The period following the return of peace and royal government in 1660 saw a resumption of the steady growth of Aberdeen (whose population would treble to 27,000 by 1800), but stagnation in Old Aberdeen. By the mid-18th century, Aberdeen was one of the ten largest towns in Scotland and England.

The appearance of the two burghs at the beginning of this period was shown in the map of 'The Newtown of Aberdeen and the Old towne of Aberdone' drawn in 1661 by Parson James Gordon of Rothiemay (see Figure 21). Superficially, little had changed for hundreds of years: the street-pattern and overall shape of both settlements seemed largely unaltered. But subtle changes were underway. In Aberdeen, as in other Scottish burghs, there was a gradual trend towards more collective, civic government. A postal service was established in 1667, street-sweeping in 1675 and in 1721 the first public lamps were introduced and a fire engine was acquired. The process culminated in the 1795 Aberdeen Police Act (which appointed thirteen commissioners to supervise services such as lighting, cleansing and water supply). In the physical environment of the burgh, the pressure of growth was leading to increasingly dense building patterns, with gardens giving way to backlands building and conversion of large dwellings into flats. This intensity was shown in far more exaggerated form on Milne's map of 1789, which followed a minor building boom of the 1760s; gardens had almost vanished beneath a network of courts, back-buildings and purpose-built tenements. The mid- and late 18th century also saw the growth of new factory-based and seaborne trade-orientated industries, based especially around the lower Don, whose steep gradient provided ample water power for early textile and paper mills. Already, the typical Aberdeen picture of a balance of industries was emerging: the majority of the town's trade was still seaborne and focused (as in the Middle Ages) on the Baltic and Netherlands.

During the 17th century and even the early/mid-18th century, older building methods – timber, thatch – still persisted, despite ineffectual bans of 1716 and 1741. But new, more permanent materials were introduced: locally made brick, for infill (for example, in gables), and pantiled or slated roofs. Most significant for the future was the spread of walling in granite, previously thought too difficult to work except for the most prestigious and expensive projects. This was used at first mostly in the form of rubble, roughly squared. The supply of building granite was greatly increased from 1730 by James Emslie's opening of Loanhead Quarry, and 1741 saw the reopening of Rubislaw Quarry by the Town Council. Although much freestone was still used, the beginnings of the architectural employment of facing granite in the 18th century coincided with the start of more 'correct'

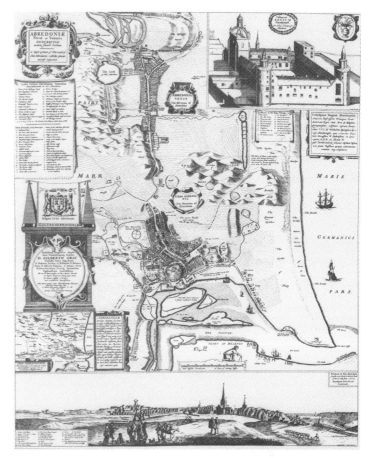

21 Map (1661) of Old Aberdeen (at top) and New Aberdeen (at bottom) by James Gordon of Rothiemay, showing the two settlements still distinct and the medieval street-pattern basically unaltered; and a model based on the map, prepared by Fenton Wyness and now housed in Provost Skene's House (City of Aberdeen Art Gallery and Museums Collections).

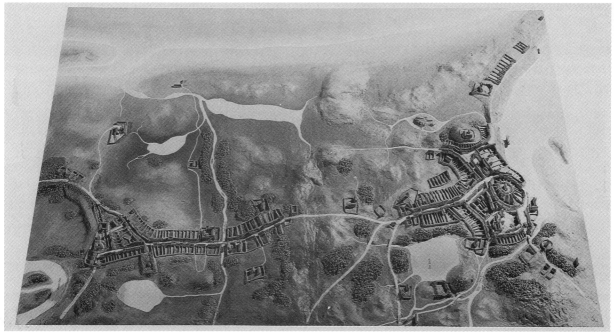

22   12–34 Broad Street, a row of mainly 18th-century stone-built houses photographed by RCAHMS in 1972 prior to clearance for the Town House Extension (1975, by City Architect Tom Watson): the tower of Peddie & Kinnear's Town House is visible at the far end (RCAHMS AB/3410).

23   Interior view (1878) of Gibbs's St Nicholas's West Church, of 1752–5 (RCAHMS AB/3909; permission to reproduce, G. Cobb).

24   Photograph taken in 1850s of St Paul's Chapel (1721, by Alexander Jaffray), the town's first Episcopalian meeting hall (RCAHMS AB/6591).

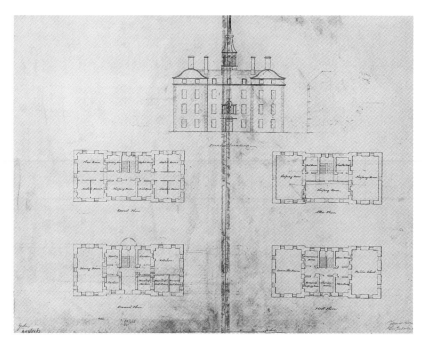

25 Robert Gordon's Hospital, built in 1730–43 by William Adam: 1907 plans and 1967 view of main staircase at second floor level (RCAHMS C21048 and AB/1160).

classical architecture, both in public buildings and in the dwellings of the rich: inside, the latter were usually panelled in wood, often with locally-made furniture and consumer goods (see Figure 22, and also Figures 122 and 123).

This was the beginning of the characteristic austere granite classicism of Aberdeen: for example, in the plain, five-bay façade of James Dun's House, Schoolhill (1767). Other major architectural monuments still employed sandstone, such as the severely geometrical rebuilt West (St Nicholas's) Church, by James Gibbs, designed in 1741 and built in 1752–5 (see Figure 23). The town's first Episcopalian meeting hall, St Paul's (1721) was altogether more humble and domestic in appearance (see Figure 24). More unusually, the mid-18th-century Seaton House (now demolished) and its estate buildings were built of handmade red bricks from the Seaton brickfields, with stone dressings.

Gradually, a range of public or secular institutions started to proliferate, designed in a classical style – ranging from the single-storeyed Old Grammar School, Schoolhill (1758; demolished c.1863) and the new Royal Infirmary at Woolmanhill (built 1739–41) to the pedimented waterhouse in Broad Street (from 1766). But an altogether new level of scale and regularity in public building was achieved in 1730–43 in Robert Gordon's Hospital, a school for fourteen boys paid for by the mortification of a rich trader formerly based in Danzig, and designed by William Adam, who had previously enlarged the Town House in 1729 (see Figure 25). Adam advised in 1730 that there should be a spacious site 'for the placement of the building, and for making the avenues large and regular, so as the whole may be decent and orderly'.[3] The grandiosely classical legacy of William Bruce's Kinross was evoked in both the austere exterior (with its attic windows) and the interior (with its traverse corridor plan);

26   Aberdeen's first 'bridge street', Marischal Street, laid out in 1766–73 as a direct route down to the harbour. Photographed by RCAHMS in 1979, prior to the demolition of the old Bannerman's Bridge and the two houses to its north, to make way for the new Inner Ring Road (RCAHMS AB/5083).

27   View of High Street, Old Aberdeen, with George Jaffray's Town House of 1788 at the far end; 1991 view. The present manicured appearance of Old Aberdeen, as, in effect, a heritage precinct within the University, results from intensive conservation work over several decades (RCAHMS B57201).

but the material was Loanhead granite. The building was occupied as a fort by the Duke of Cumberland's Hanoverian troops during the 1745–6 war, before it was eventually opened as a school.

The mid- and late 18th century was the period of the 'Aberdeen Enlightenment'; soon, the growing spirit of civic 'improvement', with its demand for classical regularity and openness, no longer contented itself with individual buildings, but began to challenge the overall form of the town, with its irregular plan and its inconveniently constricted access to the harbour and the south. Just as in contemporary Edinburgh, the bold solution seemed to be to subjugate topographical obstacles with bridges and engineering works. In 1766–73, Marischal Street, a new direct route down to the harbour, crossing Virginia Street by a bridge, was laid out (see Figure 26). Lined with merchants' houses, Marischal Street was the first in the town to be paved with granite setts, and its smooth Loanhead granite façades set new standards of classical modernity. Outside Aberdeen proper, the old ways of building still persisted. New stone houses in Old Aberdeen, such as Grant's Place (1732), were fairly low in density, while Footdee in the 1780s still comprised rows of low, thatched cottages festooned with fish and fishing gear[4] (see Figure 27). As we shall see in the next chapter, it was only following Charles Abercrombie's 1794 plan for the building of the future Union Street that the comprehensive transformation of Aberdeen into a modern industrial city would begin.

CHAPTER 4

The Neo-Classical Revolution

1800–1840

T he four decades from 1800 to 1840 were probably the most decisive and revolutionary in the history of Aberdeen. They were the years when the town's commercial and industrial modernisation, the continuing rise in population (to 63,000 in 1840) and the consequent demands for improved transport, all found outlet in a physical transformation, which was so rapid as to leave the Town Council briefly bankrupt in 1817–24 (see Figure 28).

This was a time of continuing transformation in the town's society: in the 1820s a local laird could write of 'constant revolution' in manners and social conditions over the previous decades.[5] Gradually, a broad-based civic consciousness was emerging. Politically, a Tory dominance during the first quarter of the century was succeeded, after Reform in 1832, by more shifting allegiances in municipal politics, tending towards the interests of the new middle class and supported by a vociferous local press. The work of the Aberdeen Police Commission, first established in 1795, epitomised this gradual growth in civic awareness, evolving as it did from a limited paving and lighting authority to a body prepared to intervene in wider matters of public health and order.

Industrially, this period saw the dominance of textiles in the Aberdeen economy reach its height, with a mass of factories clustered around the Green and the Don valley. At its peak in 1840, the industry employed 12,000. Agricultural industry continued its steady growth. The rise in waterborne trade prompted radical harbour improvements (successively, by Smeaton, Rennie and Telford) from 1788 onwards, as well as the building of the Aberdeenshire Canal to Inverurie in 1807 and Girdleness Lighthouse by Robert Stevenson in 1833. But the trigger for the recasting of the town itself was the improvement of the road network linking the 'improved' countryside to Aberdeen, especially following the 1795 Turnpike Act. This highlighted the inadequacy of the streets inside the town, and led the County Road Trustees to propose the construction of new streets within Aberdeen. In 1794 a plan by the County Road Surveyor, Charles Abercrombie, proposed the building of a new artery – the future Union Street – running south-east from Castlegate. Its alignment would sweep across hilly ground on brick arched viaducts, decapitating St Katherine's Hill on its north side. Another new road (King Street) would launch directly northwards from Castlegate to a new crossing of the Don, and the Ellon turnpike. The most striking element of the plan was a bridge over the deep Denburn valley, Union Bridge, which took the eventual form (after many false starts and abortive proposals) of a single-arched, 130-foot wide granite structure. It was designed by the Road Trustees' engineer, the 33-year old Thomas Fletcher, with advice from Thomas Telford.

28   Hay's 1850 perspective of Aberdeen seen from the south-east, showing the neo-classical city in its mature form, with Union Street running across from right to left, and industrial/tenemental development beginning to spread on the outskirts (RCAHMS ABD/50/3).

The proposals were approved in 1800, and the building of Union Street was begun tentatively the following year, with coordinated house designs, probably by David Hamilton. In 1807–9 large-scale building started simultaneously at both the east and the west (far) ends of the street (see Figures 29, 30 and 31, and also 11 and 125). Union Bridge was constructed in 1801–5. The building of King Street began in 1804, with unified façade designs probably by Thomas Fletcher. Subsequently, new areas on the west side of Union Bridge were laid out: for instance, Bon-Accord Terrace and Crown Street, in 1823 (see Figure 32). From 1807, too, the line of the 'Great South Road' (later Holburn Street) was fixed from the west end of Holburn Place. Other new streets included George Street, leading to the Inverurie turnpike. From 1824, gas lighting was available to light the new streets, but was only intermittently used at first.

As in the case of Edinburgh, these new arteries provided the framework on which the new, increasingly specialised institutional or 'public' buildings of the post-Improvement town could be set. In 1818 the Aberdeen-born miniature painter Andrew Robertson declared that 'the opportunity now afforded Aberdeen for the regeneration of its architecture is such as has seldom occurred in the history of any ancient city'.[6] This was also the context in which there could emerge a regional Aberdeen architectural profession. These monuments were designed above all in the monumental, Grecian style of the early 19th century by a new generation

29 View of the Castlegate and the beginning of the development of Union Street as painted by Hugh Irvine of Drum, 1803 (RCAHMS ABD/518/1).

30 Late 19th-century view of Union Street from the west, showing John Smith's churchyard screen of 1829 on the left, and the new Town House in the distance (RCAHMS B13802).

31   Aerial view (1996) of the entire length of Union Street, from the north-east (RCAHMS C56423).

32   1954 view of Bon-Accord Crescent, by Simpson, 1823 (RCAHMS AB/2623/23).

of prestigious young architects, led by John Smith (the Town's Architect) and Archibald Simpson; the first major granite monument in the city had been James Burn's Castlegate bank building of 1801 (now Bank of Scotland). Smith was the son of builder-architect William Smith, who built 44–8 Marischal Street (from 1789). Simpson, son of a merchant, began practising following his return from a tour of Italy in 1813–14. He designed a wide variety of neo-classical designs, including the porticoed Assembly Rooms for the Aberdeenshire landed classes (from 1820; now the Music Hall); the Union Buildings (Athenaeum), with their shops and reading room (1822); the austere Royal Infirmary in Woolmanhill (1832–40); and the curved New Market, with galleried interior and monumental anta-order façade, built in 1840–2 along with Market Street as part of an integrated redevelopment to clear the Putachieside slums and improve access to the harbour (see Figures 33, 34, 35 and 36, also 90, 112 and 128). Simpson's most lavish commission was heavily symbolic of the key rôle of the expanding financial services sector (banks, insurance companies, and so on) in fuelling capitalist expansion: the North of Scotland Bank at the

33   The Assembly Rooms, by Simpson (1820–2); 1991 exterior, and 1962 interior view of Music Hall (1858, by James Matthews) (RCAHMS B56019, AB/955).

35   The front façade of Simpson's New Market, 1840–2, prior to its demolition and re-development by RMJM (1971–4) (RCAHMS AB/141).

34   Archibald Simpson's Royal Infirmary building of 1832–40 in Woolmanhill; 1965 view (RCAHMS AB/602).

36   The Town School, Little Belmont Street, by John Smith (Town's Architect), 1840; 1991 view (RCAHMS B48472).

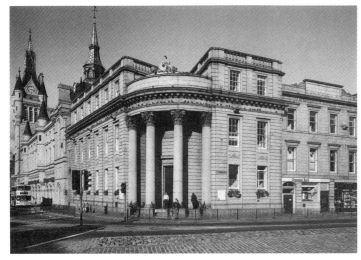

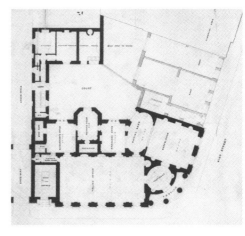

37   Simpson's North of Scotland Bank, King Street and Castlegate (1839–42), 1994 view showing Town House adjacent on the left (RCAHMS C42501); and original ground-floor plan by Simpson, in Clydesdale Bank Collection, Aberdeen City Archives (RCAHMS ABD/162/22).

38   Wall-safes in the manager's room of Archibald Simpson's Town & County Bank, 91–3 Union Street; photographed in 1970 before demolition (RCAHMS AB/2878).

angle of King Street and Castlegate (1839–42). The bank's crowning Demeter terracotta statue, by Simpson's friend James Giles, exalted the triumph of agricultural improvement in the north-east (see Figures 37 and 38, and also Figure 132).

In conformity with the 19th century's ever more sophisticated use of different historical styles to differentiate between building uses, some types, such as prisons, were thought suitable for styles other than classical architecture. For instance, James Burn's Bridewell prison (opened 1809, but later demolished) followed the castellated model of Adam's Edinburgh prototype. For collegiate buildings, English Tudor or Perpendicular styles were thought most appropriate, and were adopted by Simpson at Marischal College (1837–42). The south end of King Street featured a prominent Gothic church (Simpson's St Andrew's Episcopal, 1816) in the midst of a monumentally classical grouping, including Simpson's porticoed Medico-Chirurgical Hall of 1818–20 and Smith's North Church (1830, with Tower of the Winds steeple) (see Figure 39).

These architects' combination of modernity and neo-classical refinement was facilitated, above all, by the increasingly ubiquitous use of highly-finished granite. This was a material whose mechanised extraction and preparation, and impermeable, precise finish, symbolised Aberdeen's technological progress, especially after Alexander Macdonald's invention of granite-polishing machinery, using sand as abrasive, in 1830–1). And at the same time, through the economic importance of the large-scale granite exports (with nearly 35,000 tons per annum shipped to London by 1821, but probably most output used in the rebuilding of Aberdeen), it actually formed a key part of the town's growing industrial base. The opening of new quarries allowed greater variety of treatments or

39 West side of King Street, showing (from left) John Smith's County Record Office (1832–3), Simpson's Medico-Chirurgical Hall (1818–20) and Smith's North Church (1830); 1991 view (RCAHMS B57448).

colours – for example, Dancing Cairns granite for Simpson's Assembly Rooms portico or John Smith's St Nicholas Churchyard Screen of 1829 (see also Figure 30).

Ushering in the cult of the Granite City, commentators acclaimed the new, precise classicism, and the boldness of Union Street and Bridge. For example, Walter Thom, writing in 1811, hailed the disappearance of the gabled, pre-classical buildings which were 'giving way to more fixed rules governed by correct principles and good taste', and praised the 'primitive and simple elegance' of granite.[7]

Outside the burgh proper, improvement did not touch Old Aberdeen, but rather bypassed it, in the form of a turnpike road from King Street to the new Don Bridge (by Telford, 1827–30). But the Town Council set about the energetic 'improvement' of Footdee after 1808, by the construction (to Smith's design) of squares of two-roomed fishermen's dwellings: South Square, North Square and Middle Row (see Figures 40 and 41). An important road improvement in 1831 involved the construction of Wellington Bridge, an iron suspension bridge (by Captain S. Brown, John Gibb and John Smith) and the second crossing of the Dee, on a more direct line from the city to Stonehaven and the south.

40 Aerial view (1991) of Footdee, as rebuilt to John Smith's designs (RCAHMS B22528).

41 Girdleness Lighthouse, 1833, by Robert Stevenson (engineer to the Northern Lighthouse Board, 1799–1843); 1992 view (RCAHMS B74596).

CHAPTER 5

Religious and Municipal Grandeur

In demographic terms, the main fault-line of Aberdeen's 19th-century development ran through the 1850s, when economic difficulties slowed population growth to a trickle: emigration was a constant feature of the 19th century, especially to Canada. But the single most dramatic event of the century, in the town's civic and social life, occurred in 1843: the Disruption of the Church of Scotland, which reinvigorated the spiritual dimension in the city's development, hitherto moulded exclusively by the materialistic dynamic of 'improvement'. The Disruption, a schism in which a large anti-Erastian faction (opposed to state control) separated from the Kirk and formed the rival Free Church of Scotland, hit Aberdeen with a force unmatched in any other major urban centre – perhaps because old-fashioned patronage had already all but disappeared from the town by the 1830s. All fifteen of the town's ministers, and the great bulk of their congregations, seceded, leaving the existing churches virtually empty. The architectural consequence of the Disruption was a great tide of competitive church-building spanning half a century, which refined Aberdeen's image as a romantic classical city by adding tall steeples (usually Gothic) to the Grecian horizontality of its secular architecture.

The first building drive was focused on the temporary wooden churches built by the Free Church immediately following the Disruption: the Free Church was dominated by the entrepreneurial middle classes, so building finance constituted little obstacle. For example, when Dr Alexander Spence, minister of St Clement's Parish Church – a key participant in the Disruption events in Edinburgh – returned to Aberdeen shortly afterwards, he found that a new wooden church had already been built ready for him in Summer Lane by his seceding congregation; most of the work had been carried out in a single night. Next followed the rapid and economical building in stone of the first permanent Free churches. A new stone-built St Clement's, for instance, was built in Prince Regent Street by October 1843. Of these new buildings, the most dominant, in situation and architecture, was Simpson's lofty brick-spired 'Triple Kirks' above the Denburn Valley, built in 1843–4 for the seceding east, west and south congregations at a cost of just over £6,000. The final stage in the religious building frenzy unleashed by the Disruption was the erection, over the last quarter of the century, of many permanent churches of a grandly granite-built character. Generally, their locations followed the movement of the bourgeoisie from the centre out to new western suburbs. In the 1870s and 1880s the Free Church embarked on an extension movement, with projects such as Pirie & Clyne's idiosyncratic Gothic Queen's Cross Free Church of 1880–1 (its first minister the charismatic preacher and theologian Dr George Adam Smith) (see Figure 42). Later followed churches such as Brown & Watt's

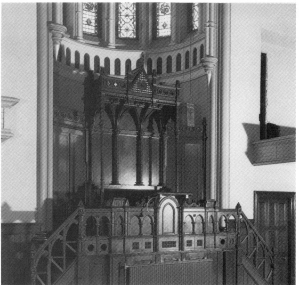

42   Pirie & Clyne's Queen's Cross Free Church,
1880–1: 1991 view (RCAHMS B48466).

43   Carden Place United Presbyterian Church,
by Ellis & Wilson, 1880–2: exterior and interior
views (RCAHMS B05935, B05940)

soaring, Gothic Beechgrove (1896–1900) and Holburn (1893–4), or classical Melville (1901–3).

The rival denominations responded in kind. The United Presbyterians (another wealthy, middle-class grouping, which united with the Free Church in 1900) built the massive Carden Place Church in 1880–2; the architect, R. G. Wilson, was an elder of its congregation (see Figure 43). The Established Church, which saw a great recovery in the city in the later 19th century, set up its own Church Extension Association, and built west-end parish churches such as Rubislaw (opened 1875, by J. R. Mackenzie) or Mannofield (1882, by Jenkins & Marr). Outside the Presbyterian mainstream, there was also much activity. The Catholics, under Bishop James Kyle, built St Mary's Church (later Cathedral) in 1860, to the designs of Alexander Ellis, with a later spire by Robert Wilson; and the Episcopalians commissioned H. O. Tarbolton's grandiosely austere St Peter's, Torry (1898). A special Episcopalian project was the mission church of St Margaret of Scotland, built up by Rev. John Comper from 1870; it was enlarged from 1887 by Comper's architect son, Ninian.

In parallel with these religious developments, the mid- and late 19th century also saw dramatic changes in the secular life of the city. There was, however, no equivalent to the intense industrial or social specialisation seen on Clydeside and in Dundee, and there remained a relatively large service and professional sector – including architecture. Here designers trained by Smith and Simpson, such as William Smith, Thomas Mackenzie, and James Matthews, established dominance, and in turn trained the next generation of the late 19th century (including A. Marshall Mackenzie, son of Thomas, and William Kelly, architectural heir of William Smith).

During an economic crisis in the 1840s and 1850s, the city's textile industry largely collapsed, leaving only a few large survivors such as the Broadford Works of Messrs Richards (linen) and J. & J. Crombie's Grandholm Works (wool) (see Figures 44 and 45). In replacement of textiles, a far more balanced and diversified range of newer industries

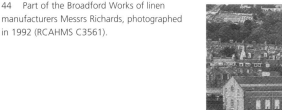
44   Part of the Broadford Works of linen manufacturers Messrs Richards, photographed in 1992 (RCAHMS C3561).

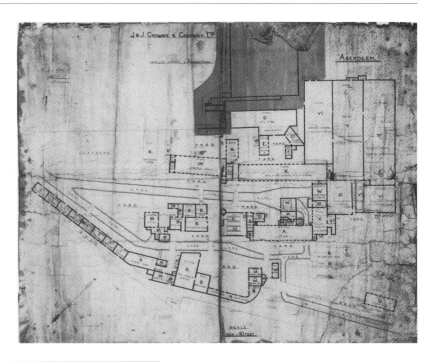

45 Grandholm Mills (J. & J. Crombie), 1891 plan of works (RCAHMS B50401); cloth scouring in Building 27, c. 1930s (B50274); and 1965 view of Bolton Corliss engine (RCAHMS AB/183).

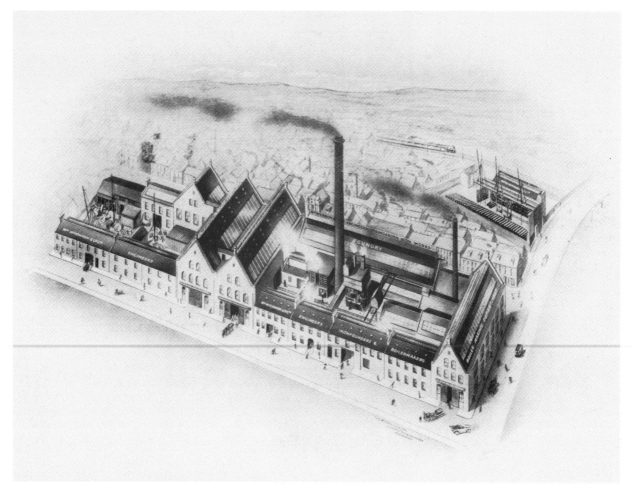

46   Spring Garden Iron Works (W McKinnon &
Co.), view of site from south-east before
construction of new offices in c.1908; extract
from early catalogue.

emerged, and rapid population growth resumed – from 74,000 in 1861 to
164,000 fifty years later (see Figures 46, 47 and 48). The town's new
industries swung decisively towards its own natural hinterland resources
and materials. The first to be exploited was the land, or, more precisely, the
produce of the north-east's now mature agricultural revolution: a vast
cattle-exporting industry had grown up by the 1850s. The sea, too, offered
obvious opportunities: the 1850s–70s saw a boom in shipbuilding,
especially of sail-powered clippers, while the years after 1882 witnessed the
meteoric rise of fishing, using steam trawlers, as the city's major industry
(see Figure 49). By 1909 Aberdeen commanded half of the Scottish white
fish market, and between the wars as many as 360 boats operated out of
Aberdeen (see also Figure 102).

In parallel to these developments, and the general expansion of
shipboard and entrepôt trade, radical improvements were made to the
harbour in the mid-19th century. The Board of Management/
Commissioners (established in 1829) embarked on a massive programme
of remodelling, involving construction of a new tidal dock, new fish
markets round the Albert Basin and, in 1871–3, the diversion of the Dee
(see Figures 50 and 51). By 1850, of course, transportation of commodities

47   Spring Garden Iron Works, 1992 view of castings ready to be finished in machine shop (RCAHMS B74809).

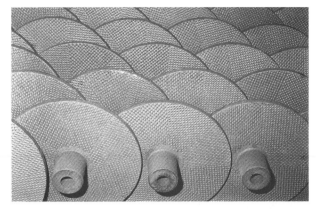

48   Sandilands Chemical Works, group photograph of workers and tools, c. 1900 (RCAHMS A80537).

49   Hall Russell Shipyard, 1989 view along west side of building hall, showing Ship No.1000 (a welded-steel, twin-screw cargo-passenger ferry for the St Helena service) under construction (RCAHMS B17858).

50   View of Aberdeen from Torry in *c.* 1878, showing the diverted course of the Dee and the newly completed Town House steeple (RCAHMS AB/3918; permission to reproduce, G. Cobb).

51   Regent Shed, a two-storey, steel-framed transit block built in 1898 and 1906 to the designs of R. G. Nicol, Harbour Engineer; photographed in 1983 prior to demolition (RCAHMS A7231).

such as cattle had been revolutionised by the arrival of the railway in Aberdeen, allowing fresh fish and cattle transport to England; yet harbour traffic tonnage nevertheless doubled from 1860 to 1900. Railway development continued with the building of the Aberdeen-based Great North of Scotland Railway (from 1854), and the opening of the arched-roof Joint Station (designed by William Smith) and Denburn Valley link line in 1866–7 (designed by John Willet) (see also Figure 65).

The industry most directly bound up with the built environment was, naturally, granite: here the preeminence of Rubislaw was challenged by John Fyfe's new Kemnay quarry, opened in 1858. Aberdeenshire quarrying reached its all-time maximum output in 1898, and in 1900, the granite firms achieved a peak of prestige, with the patronage of Queen Victoria in projects such as the royal mausolea at Frogmore, and a peak of economic importance, with a workforce of 2,700 in the city itself, engaged in largely steam-powered quarrying (above all at Rubislaw) and polishing operations (see Figures 52 and 53). 70,000 tons of finished granite were exported annually, especially to the United States; Aberdeenshire quarriers and

52   Rubislaw Quarry, late 19th-century view (RCAHMS AB/7275; permission to reproduce, Richard Emerson), and 1989 aerial view after closure (RCAHMS B22279).

53   Rubislaw Quarry, mid-20th-century plan (P. B. Enfield, *The Granite Industry of Aberdeen*, 1951).

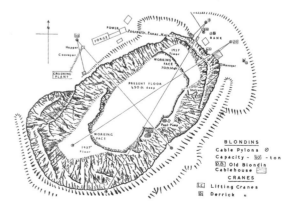

masons also found much employment, temporary and permanent, in the United States. But an even more important outlet for granite production was the development of Aberdeen itself; for this was the period when the 'Granite City', as an entity, was created. If Scotland was unique in 19th-century Europe in its use of high-quality facing stone as the material for the construction of the mass capitalist city, Aberdeen was unique in Scotland in its use of impermeable granite for this purpose, for the building not just of public monuments but of the background buildings, the ordinary homes of rich and poor alike. In 1907 the granite industry's historian, W. Diack, could boast that its rise was 'one of the romances of Scottish history'; across the world, 'sarcophagi of Aberdeenshire granite hold the dust of kings and emperors'.[8] But by that time the industry was already in steep decline, its top-quality deposits already worked out and its principal customer, the speculative housebuilder, in retreat.

The late 19th century was the era of the relentless spread of the residential suburb, its uniform 'terraces' of middle-class dwellings or working-class tenements built and rented out in unplanned fashion by myriad small speculators (see also Figures 66, 107 and 127). Before the 1880s, Aberdeen was still a relatively compact city, with a degree of social mix. Now, a far more pronounced class segregation by geographical location became the rule. The typical Aberdeen tenement, with its high attic, used an unusually large amount of timber internally, especially in its staircase, but the external face was one of granite severity. Some three-storeyed Aberdeen housing comprised two-floored upper flats above single-floor dwellings on the ground floor. Occasional quirky variants on the housing theme, such as Pirie & Clyne's incised, Thomson-like detailing at Hamilton Place and Argyll Place (both early 1880s) only underlined the general homogeneity (see Figure 54). Late 19th-century developments of villas of the wealthy in streets such as Queen's Road or Rubislaw Den North and South were also in granite, and avoided the extremes of opulence of Dundee or Glasgow. But the villa still allowed, in comparison to terraces, a more individualistic architectural expression, at the hands of architects such as George Coutts or Arthur Clyne (see Figures 55, 56, 57, 58 and 59, and also 106 and 133). The final speculative building boom peaked in 1899, when 450 dwellings were completed; by 1908, due to the nationwide prewar building slump, the completion rate was a mere 60, and the building and granite industries were 'very depressed'.[9]

This residential expansion was underlined and facilitated by the vast municipal boundary extension of 1891, which took in Old Aberdeen and Woodside, as well as the booming, industrial suburb of Torry, south of the Dee and densely developed with tenements since 1883; in 1899 the town became a largely self-governing city, or County of City. But the most spectacular architectural expression of the municipal pride of the new, expansionist Aberdeen had already been achieved in 1867–73, when a new centre of civic government – the County and Municipal Buildings, designed by Peddie & Kinnear – had been built at a cost of £50,000. This grand monument of municipal assertion, which monumentally renewed the 'hearth-stone of the burgh', evoked a Baronial imagery of 'royal Deeside' in its architectural style and 60 m high bartizaned tower, while its

54   50 Queen's Road, 1886, by Pirie & Clyne; one of the most idiosyncratic of that practice's forceful and eclectic works; 1991 detail view (RCAHMS B48286).

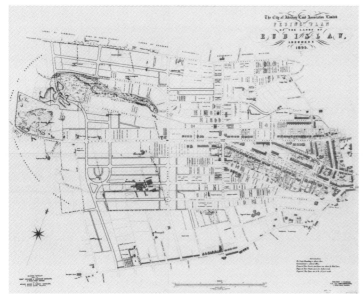

56 Elevations, block plan, section of middle-class row-house in Bon-Accord Street, 1891 (RCAHMS C21219)

58 Aerial view (1989) of the junction of Rubislaw Den North and Forest Road, showing the low density of this villa suburb (RCAHMS B22272).

55 Unexecuted 1895 feuing plan of the lands of Rubislaw: the future Anderson Drive is shown on its present-day alignment at the left-hand side (RCAHMS C21199).

57 1 Rubislaw Den North, 1909, by George Coutts: 'Old English' style in pink granite (RCAHMS B56440).

59 The Chalet, 4 Anderson Drive, 1904, by G. Fordyce: 1991 view. A more luxurious precursor of the city's ubiquitous single-storeyed interwar bungalows (RCAHMS B56421).

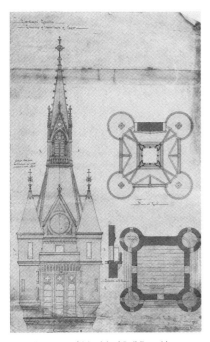

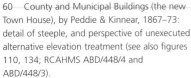

60   County and Municipal Buildings (the new Town House), by Peddie & Kinnear, 1867–73: detail of steeple, and perspective of unexecuted alternative elevation treatment (see also figures 110, 134; RCAHMS ABD/448/4 and ABD/448/3).

stonework exemplified a refined granite modernity[10] (see Figure 60, and also 110).

More and more, the civic authorities (the Town Council, and the Commissioners of Police, amalgamated in 1871) intervened to regulate the services of the modern large town, spurred on by fear of cholera and other threats to bourgeois health and order; these interventions increased in the 1880s, when the council was a bastion of Liberal Party power. Capitalists and professionals such as the lawyer Sir Alexander Anderson or the shipowner George Thompson entered the Town Council and pressed for a range of new municipal enterprises. Filtered river water was secured through an aqueduct supply by the Police Commissioners from Cairnton (Invercannie), 19 miles up the Dee, from 1866, and extended from 1885. Sewage was reorganised in 1866–70 by the Commissioners of Police. Bridge-building included the 1881 Victoria Bridge linking the town to Torry. Public parks began with Victoria Park, in 1871. Gas was municipalised and expanded in 1871, and Scotland's largest gasholder was built at Gallowhills in 1892–4 (see Figure 61). Education, in the wake of the 1872 Education Act, saw energetic building by the School Board and a rise in their rolls from 8,000 pupils in 1882 to 26,000 in 1904 (see Figures 62 and 63). Electricity was supplied by the Corporation from 1894, and augmented by a large new power station at Millburn Street (built in 1901–3) (see Figure 64). Transportation was served by municipalisation and electrification of the private tramway system in 1898. Health innovations included the Town Council's construction of the Epidemic, or City, Hospital in 1874; the building of the Kingseat Asylum on the dispersed 'colony' plan by the City District Lunacy Board, in 1901–4; and the building of the Oldmill Poorhouse for the 'aged and respectable poor' on 1906–7. In 1903 W. Watt's celebratory paper, *A Century in Aberdeen*,

61　Gallowhills Gas Holder, 1892–4: the largest in the country at its construction, 1991 view of lifting mechanism (RCAHMS B45989).

62　Ashley Road School, 1887, by Jenkins & Marr; 1992 view (RCAHMS B70410).

63　Kittybrewster Primary School, Great Northern Road, built between 1897 and 1900 by Brown & Watt, to accommodate 1,100 children: façade detail, showing the superb standard of granite work applied even to everyday public buildings by the turn of the century (RCAHMS B55678).

64　Art Nouveau ventilator in Justicemill Lane, serving the cable subway built by Aberdeen Corporation in connection with Millburn Street Power Station (1901–3); 1991 view (RCAHMS B55078).

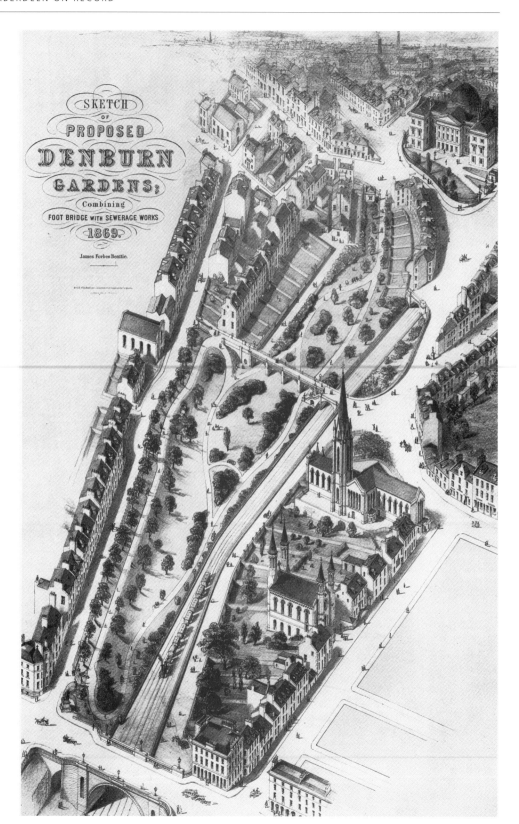

65   Perspective 1869 by J. F. Beattie showing proposed Denburn Gardens. Although the railway, the 'Triple Kirks', and the Congregational Church are much as today, a clutter of 18th- and early 19th-century buildings still occupies the area later to be cleared away for the grand civic ensemble of Rosemount Viaduct (RCAHMS ABD/63/2).

66 Urquhart Road, view of typical 1890s three- and four-storeyed granite-built tenements, showing (on the right) the ubiquitous Aberdeen top-floor mansard storey, and (on the left), Aberdeen Corporation's first housing scheme, built in 1897 (RCAHMS B55654).

declared that 'a great process of "municipalisation" has been going on'.[11]

Some areas still remained a preserve of private or voluntary action: for example, 1870 saw the foundation of the Association for Improving the Condition of the Poor (renamed the Aberdeen Association for Social Service in 1947). And there was little sign yet of concern in what would become the major area of municipal action in the 20th century: housing. Just as Aberdeen avoided extremes of wealth, so it also avoided extremes of dense slum housing; far fewer lived in one- or two-roomed dwellings than in Glasgow or Dundee. This obviated any need for massive City Improvement reconstruction schemes in the centre, although there was some municipal clearance around Castlehill and Gallowgate, as well as slum demolition through railway construction (see also Figure 130). A limited scheme of 1886–97 at the west end of Schoolhill was pushed through by the architect and Lord Provost, James Matthews. This resulted in the construction of a new civic group of buildings at the north end of Union Terrace (including a library, theatre and United Free church), and the building of another spectacular 'bridge-street', here on a curved alignment: Rosemount Viaduct, with its high, flanking tenements (see Figure 65). The Town Council began its first tentative experiments in direct housing provision, with the construction of a model lodging house in East North Street (1896), and sixteen tenements of one- and two-roomed flats in Urquhart and Park Roads in 1897 (see Figure 66).

67   Marischal College Extension, 1893-1906, by A. Marshall Mackenzie; 1994 views of main staircase and new west façade (see also figures 136, 137; RCAHMS C16659 and 16641).

68   Aerial view (1996) of the east end of Union Street and Castlegate, showing Marischal College and the Town House complex (at centre) and the Castlehill multi-storey Corporation housing blocks of 1965–8 at upper right (RCAHMS C56412).

69 Rosemount Viaduct, seen in 1892 following the completion of most of the City Improvement scheme. From left to right: statue of Wallace, 1888, by W. Grant Stevenson; Public Library, 1891–2, by Brown & Watt; South United Free Church, 1892, by A. Marshall Mackenzie; His Majesty's Theatre, 1904–8, by F. Matcham (RCAHMS AB/3525).

The drive to build new public buildings in granite culminated in 1893–1906, when the recently unified (1858) University of Aberdeen, fuelled by a bequest from Charles Mitchell, embarked on a vast expansion of the Marischal College site, to A. Marshall Mackenzie's designs. The scheme included a massive examination hall and the 80 m high Mitchell Tower, as well as the demolition and replacement of the medieval Greyfriars Kirk (in 1903), following the city's rejection of preservationist lobbying. The 'Skyscraper Perpendicular' Gothic style of the complex was loosely inspired by Simpson's original Marischal College group, but also resembled the verticalised collegiate style then increasingly in vogue for universities in the United States. The bristling array of Kemnay granite – the second largest granite building in Europe (after the Escorial) – was later hailed by W. Diack as 'a testimony to the superb durability of our Aberdeenshire granite, and the pride of our silver city by the sea'[12] (see Figures 67 and 68). At a very different scale, but with equal civic pride, June 1888 saw the unveiling of William Grant Stevenson's Wallace Statue at Rosemount Viaduct, paid for by John Steill, its base of 'massive rough blocks of Corrennie granite' supporting a figure of 'the hero standing facing the south in a boldly erect, vigorous and life-like attitude'. At the ceremony, the Marquis of Lorne hailed the statue as a symbol of British imperial prowess: 'a united people, the richest and yet the most warlike of our time'.[13] (see Figure 69).

CHAPTER 6

The Wartime and Interwar Years

1914–1939

The years after World War I saw growing challenges to the certainties that had governed Aberdeen's 19th-century development. Socially and economically, there was growing discontent with *laissez-faire* capitalism, and a demand for a more disciplined, collective interpretation of modernity. Despite the flourishing of organisations such as the Northern Co-operative Society (founded 1861), it rapidly became clear that the state, and especially local authorities, would have to take the lead rôle in this strategy. However, despite a growing socialist presence, Aberdeen Town Council was still governed by 'non-political' ratepayer groups.

Architecturally, the individualism of the 19th century, and its expression of new building types through different recipes of historical 'styles', was now rejected. The general international revolt from late 19th-century ornateness towards the 20th-century emphasis on 'simplicity' was more complicated in Aberdeen, owing to the relative sobriety of 19th-century granite architecture. Self-styled 'Traditionalist' architects such as William Kelly modified the cult of Aberdeen granite monumentality, downplaying the emphasis on classicism and precision in favour of more abstract socio-

70 A. Marshall Mackenzie's War Memorial and Cowdray Hall, opened 1925; 1991 view (RCAHMS B57427).

architectural ideals such as 'fitness' or 'craftsmanship', or neo-medieval conceptions of folk community.[14] Classical buildings, such as Marshall Mackenzie's War Memorial and Cowdray Hall (opened 1925) became increasingly sober in appearance (see Figures 70 and 71, and also 101 and 131).

Although the worst extremes of depression experienced on Clydeside were avoided, the economic picture in interwar Aberdeen was, on the whole, one of stagnation. At first, some industries continued to thrive: 1925 saw an all-time record for the total weight of fish landed at Aberdeen (130,000 tons). The granite industry was increasingly troubled: annual exports in 1930 were less than 15 per cent of the 1909 level, although granite-building within the city experienced something of a revival from its pre-1914 slump. The role of private enterprise agencies in the building development of the city was only gradually curtailed. New fields for entrepreneurial building zeal included the proliferation of entertainment and consumer buildings. Prewar years had already seen building of some specialised recreational and commercial buildings. Pittodrie Park football stadium opened in 1899 (followed four years later by the foundation of Aberdeen Football Club) (see Figure 72). Following the first showing of 'animated photographs' in 1896 (in the Music Hall) and the opening of a cinema in a converted building in 1908 (the Gaiety), 1914 saw the opening of the city's first purpose-built cinema, La Scala, 234 Union Street (designed in 'Mediterranean' style by John Ednie of Glasgow and George Sutherland of Aberdeen); the city's first F. W. Woolworth multiple store also opened in that year. Other interwar places of entertainment included an ice rink and dog track (later war damaged) at Garthdee (see Figure 73).

71   Commercial Bank, Union Street, 1936, by Jenkins & Marr: Aberdeen's representative example of the interwar Beaux-Arts style of commercial palazzo (RCAHMS B39545).

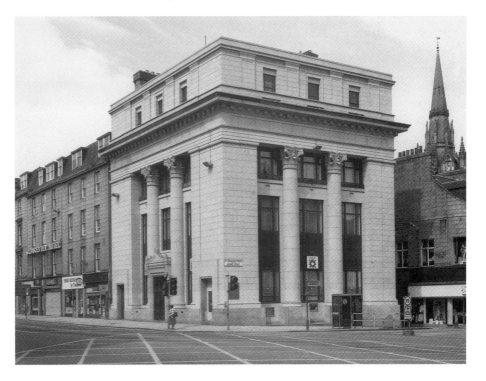

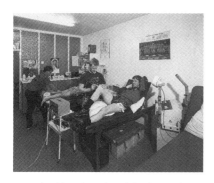

72   Pittodrie Park Stadium (Aberdeen F C), physiotherapy room: part of a comprehensive 1992 survey of the stadium (RCAHMS B57989).

73   The main entrance of the Art Deco Northern Hotel, 1937–8, by A. G. R. Mackenzie; 1991 view. Mackenzie later played a major rôle in the first postwar historic-buildings listing programme in the north-east (RCAHMS B55683).

Private suburban housing development, increasingly for sale rather than rent, continued on a fairly extensive scale. By 1939 nearly 5,000 dwellings (mostly still in granite) had been built in areas such as King's Gate and Angusfield by speculative developers, including the flamboyant anti-socialist, Tom Scott Sutherland (who began speculative housebuilding in 1926–7). The boom in motor transport, with municipal bus services commencing in 1921, and 5,500 private cars licensed in Aberdeen by 1938, encouraged the building of single-storeyed dwellings individually distributed in the form of bungalows, rather than vertically stacked in tenements (see also Figure 59).

Increasingly, social building projects played a more prominent rôle, and for these, the new predilection for 'non-stylistic' cubic granite architectural forms seemed appropriate. Social buildings designed by the staff of City Architect (1924–54) Alexander Gardner in this manner included Bon-Accord Baths (opened 1940) and Kaimhill Crematorium (1937) (see Figure 74). The new city Education Authority was created in 1919 and the beginning of nursery school provision in 1933. Building in the field of health was dominated by the Joint Hospitals scheme of 1927–36, inspired by a 1920 proposal by Professor Matthew Hay for concentration of all Aberdeen hospitals on a single 17-acre site. Its £525,000 cost financed partly through a vast fund-raising campaign across the north-east, the new Foresterhill complex comprised premises for the Aberdeen Royal Infirmary, Maternity Hospital and medical school buildings. It was mostly designed by William Kelly's partner, James B. Nicol, in an austere, flat-roofed classical manner, and constructed (owing to public demand) in granite; the 'spacious and airy' plan comprised an east–west spine, with ward spurs running south[15] (see Figures 75 and 76). A new Sick Children's Hospital was built nearby, slightly earlier, to Kelly's designs (1926–8); after the war, in 1955, the main hospital group was extended eastwards in the same style.

But the focus of social architecture was the rapidly growing programme of housebuilding by the Town Council, which produced nearly 6,500 houses between 1919 and 1939 – 30 per cent higher than the private building total. Not only was the Corporation's total debt in 1938 five times higher than in 1902, but 40 per cent of the total was accounted for by provision of housing – an almost non-existent commitment in 1902. The prewar difficulties of private housing had been compounded by the imposition of rent controls from 1915, which effectively suffocated the old system of private speculative provision, for skilled workers as well as for the middle classes. The results of this were growing shortages of new houses, overcrowding, and an un-improved or deteriorating housing stock. By 1938, Aberdeen was especially unusual among Scottish cities in the number of dwellings without individual water supply (4,903, compared to only 219 in Glasgow). Answering the call of the 1917 Ballantyne Report on working-class housing (and subsequent government legislation), that the state should seize control of social housing

74 Bon-Accord Baths, designed by the City Architect's Department and opened in 1940; views of granite exterior (1992, RCAHMS B55079) and concrete-arched interior (1994, RCAHMS C43000).

75 Aberdeen Royal Infirmary, Foresterhill (1927–36); 1992 view of granite ward blocks designed by James B. Nicol (RCAHMS B70408).

76 Foresterhill Hospital complex, 1989 aerial view, including the cubic granite blocks of the 1927–36 Joint Hospitals Scheme at centre and bottom left, and the multi-storey racetrack block of the 1960s at bottom right (RCAHMS B22269).

77   Rosemount Square (1938–46 Corporation housing scheme); 1992 view of main entrance with T. B. Huxley Jones sculpture above (RCAHMS B70434).

provision, Aberdeen Town Council began, gradually, to build houses for rent. This programme started with cottage housing schemes such as Torry Garden City (by Kelly, as Director of Housing, after 1919), but increasingly, in the 1930s, concentrating on the building of tenements for relief of overcrowding or slum-clearance (as at Woodside and Powis): 2,955 houses were demolished as slums between 1919 and 1939. The greatest boost to municipal output came, ironically, from speculative housebuilder Scott Sutherland, who joined the council in 1934 and became Housing Convener two years later: municipal output reached a maximum of 1016 in 1938 (see also Figure 121). Within this low-cost field of building, construction in granite became steadily more costly, and was confined to 'all-granite' schemes like the tenemental Powis (1939) and the dramatic Art Deco Rosemount Square (1938–46), whose sweepingly curved courtyard plan echoed the Viennese municipal housing of the 1920s, and which was adorned by stylised sculptures of the elements by T. B. Huxley Jones (see Figure 77).

From the 1920s the demand for state intervention and control in the built environment, especially in housing, was often summed up in the one

78   Model of 1937 competition-winning scheme for Kincorth, by Clifford Holliday, Robert Gardner-Medwin and Denis Winston; the scheme was eventually built on a similar, but somewhat more conservative layout.

79   Arbroath Way, Kincorth, showing granite houses built in the 1950s, and a 14-storey point block added in 1963-4; 1991 view (RCAHMS B56123).

word, 'planning'. The city boundaries were once again extended in 1934, to a total (11,000 acres) four times the 1891 area. But now it was not simply enough to allow new suburbs to grow haphazardly; housing should take the form of 'planned communities' or even of 'satellite towns' separated from industry, and spaciously laid out in greenery. Here Aberdeen, with its passion for civic order, was an early innovator. Following permissive government legislation in 1925, a joint committee was established by the Corporation, along with Kincardineshire and Aberdeenshire County Councils, and a town-planning scheme covering the city and immediate hinterland was set up in 1933, largely through the persuasion of the joint committee convener, Henry Alexander. In addition to controls on the 'density' and general form of all new development in the area, and the establishment of the principle of a green belt surrounding the city, there was a more ambitious aim to plan a 34-mile strategic road network of ring and radial roads linking new settlements. An international competition for the first of these settlements, a 'satellite township' at Kincorth, was won in 1937 by London architects Clifford Holliday, Robert Gardner-Medwin and Denis Winston. Their scheme combined a generally Garden City layout with a hilltop community sector and a degree of traffic segregation; a simplified version, retaining granite as the basic building material, was built after the war[16] (see Figures 78 and 79).

CHAPTER 7

Welfare State to Oil Boom

Whereas World War I had left Aberdeen undamaged, the second conflict, with thirty-four air raids, saw considerable damage: the worst raid, on 21 April 1943, destroyed 599 houses (see also Figure 117). After 1945 some military and civil defence activity continued in connection with the Cold War, but most attention turned to civil rebuilding (see Figure 80). Boosted even further by the great collective 'war effort' of 1939–45, the ethos of state-directed planning reached its climax across Scotland in a succession of 1940s regional and city plans. Whereas many of these contained radical proposals of reconstruction, the Aberdeen city plan *Granite City* (1952), prepared by consultant planners W. Dobson Chapman and Charles F. Riley, was rather unusual in the emphasis it placed on continuity. Its obvious reverence for classical Aberdeen was clear not least in its title, and in its cover, which portrayed patterning on a slab of stone. *Granite City's* plans for the city-region were largely an elaboration of the prewar framework of strategic roads, zoning of uses, green belt, and satellite communities. Even in its proposal for the staged re-development of the city centre on regularised Beaux-Arts lines, with an inner ring road and green spaces around, all the major streets and monuments of the neo-classical era were to be preserved. Unlike overcrowded Glasgow, there was to be no mass overspill of population and industry: the existing balance of industries was seen as satisfactory,

80 UK Warning and Monitoring Organisation underground control room, Quarry Road, 1992 view; one of a series of surveillance bunkers intended to track nuclear attacks, but closed down in the 1990s (RCAHMS B742).

81 'Orlit' experimental 1940s concrete blockwork houses, Garthdee housing scheme (Sam Bunton, architect); 1988 view (RCAHMS A80441).

and population was, if anything, to rise slightly. The total population of the city (within its pre-1975 boundaries) would reach a maximum of 186,000 in 1963. The preface of *Granite City* boasted that with relatively little change, Aberdeen could become 'the planner's specification for an "ideal city"'.[17]

The reality of early postwar building was different from these plans. As elsewhere in Scotland, there was almost total concentration on constructing large numbers of council houses, now for 'general needs' rather than the poor. The speculative builder was kept out of the way by government curbs, and the city's big private builders (Alexander Hall & Sons, W. J. Anderson and Peter Cameron) were yoked, as contractors, to the Corporation's building drive. From 1945 the council was predominantly controlled by the Labour Party, but there was a consensus with the Progressives (non-socialists) on the need for municipal housing (see Figure 81). For most of the 1950s and 1960s, the Housing Committee was chaired by Labour councillors such as Robert S. Lennox (later City Treasurer), Norman Hogg or Jock Greig; but sometimes the flamboyant Tory 'Battling Baillie', Frank Magee, held the post. At first, most council housing comprised cottages and low flats, in large new suburban schemes such as Mastrick and Northfield, with efforts to build collective facilities such as community centres (beginning with Powis in 1941, in a converted 19th-century Baronial house). Rising costs further squeezed the use of granite; after the mid-1950s, the use of synthetic granite 'Fyfestone' blocks began to spread, as a substitute (see also Figure 79).

From the late 1950s, with land shortages in prospect, the city began to look to the more radical solution of housing in the form of multi-storey blocks. This signalled, for the first time, an architectural break from Traditionalist ideas of 'craftsmanlike' granite sobriety towards the cosmopolitan and assertively new forms of the International Modern

82   Corporation's Ashgrove housing scheme, including old people's houses (foreground) and 10-storey tower block (the first in the city) of 1959; 1991 view (RCAHMS B39983).

83   Aerial view (1989) of Tillydrone-Hayton housing scheme, including the 14- and 19-storey tower blocks built in 1964–8 (RCAHMS B22248).

Movement – a movement, led in Scotland by Robert Matthew, which took the vertical 'tower block' as its emblem.

Following 1959 visits to Glasgow and the pioneering London County Council scheme at Roehampton, the Housing Committee embarked on a two-pronged multi-storey building campaign. Unlike most central-belt towns, where the design-and-build 'package deal' reigned supreme, in Aberdeen almost all designs were by the staff of George McI. Keith, City Architect from 1954 to 1970. The first element in the campaign was the building of tower blocks in the suburbs, beginning at Ashgrove (1959–61) and Hazlehead (1962–3), and building up to large groups at Tillydrone-Hayton (1964–8), Cornhill-Stockethill (1966–8), and Seaton (1968–74; including 1,247 high flats) (see Figures 82 and 83). The other element comprised larger 'slab' blocks built on clearance sites, beginning with Chapel Street/Skene Street (1961), Gallowgate and Castlehill (from 1965) and culminating in the massive slabs of Hutcheon Street (1973) (see Figure 84). Following this multi-storey programme, in which, due to careful management, few of the problems of unpopularity or physical damage of other cities were encountered, the Corporation's 'waiting list' for housing

84 Gallowgate multi-storey re-development area, 1965–6, designed by the City Architect's Department; 1986 view (RCAHMS A42195).

85 Late 1960s Corporation low-rise terraces and flats, Balnagask South development; 1991 view (RCAHMS B48496).

86 Aerial view (1989) of Sheddocksley housing development: Corporation low-rise housing of the 1970s, using modified Radburn layouts (RCAHMS B22285).

87 'The Hillocks' development, Bucksburn, 1965–8; 1992 view. A scheme of housing built by Aberdeenshire County Council (on a site which was at that time beyond the city boundaries) as a design-and-build 'package-deal' by Wimpey. The photograph shows the 'Radburn'-style segregation of pedestrian and vehicular access (RCAHMS B70442).

plummeted (from 7,300 in 1961 to 3,700 ten years later). By 1971 nearly one-third of the total housing stock of the city had been built since 1951, and almost half of the city's houses were owned by local or other public authorities (see Figures 85, 86 and 87). In 1977 the Director of Planning, William Colclough, argued that high buildings 'can be said to have considerable dramatic effect seen from many viewpoints outside and within the city, particularly when they catch and reflect brilliant sunshine, burn with the reds and purples of evening sunsets or appear softly indistinct through the haze'. However, he admitted that 'some would hold a less fulsome opinion'.[18] The final phase of multi-storey housebuilding, unique to Aberdeen, was a specialised programme of sheltered blocks for the elderly (the last, at Jasmine Place, being completed in 1985) (see Figure 88).

In other areas of building, the 1960s and 1970s had also seen a boom in the Modernist solution of geometrical tall blocks on open-plan layouts. Development of the Foresterhill hospital site continued from 1963 with the erection of a multi-storey 'racetrack' block (containing wards in a ring around a service core), while the west side of Broad Street was re-developed

88   Jasmine Place, 11-storey block of old people's sheltered housing units built in 1984–5 by Aberdeen District Council; 1986 views of exterior and commemorative plaque. This tower, constructed by Wimpey, was the last high-rise council block built in Scotland (RCAHMS A42212, 42213).

in 1965 with a tall slab block of council offices, St Nicholas House (see also Figures 15 and 76). The University's prewar stagnation was now dramatically reversed, with a tripling of student numbers in the 1960s alone; its development plan, drawn up after 1957 by Robert Matthew (who himself designed Crombie Hall, 1955–60, Scotland's first mixed hall of residence), included construction of several multi-storey slab blocks. One or two other developments, although avoiding high blocks, were even more novel in their plans. One of the most striking was the rippling, mound-like profile of Covell Matthews's Northern Co-operative store, George Street (1966). The new Gray's School of Art, at Garthdee (1964–6) by D. Michael Shewan, was a complete contrast in its Miesian sobriety (see Figures 89, 90 and 91, and also Figure 25).

By the mid- and late 1960s, the architectural emphasis was shifting slowly away from large-scale Modernist developments of towers and slabs in open space – just as, in society as a whole, the concepts of mass, state-directed modernity were being rejected, by many, as rigid and dictatorial. A precocious conservationist agitator was Fenton Wyness, who as early as 1961 had attacked the 'degradation' of Union Street by postwar re-development.[19] In reflection of government policy, from the late 1960s the

89 Crombie Hall, University of Aberdeen, 1955–60, by Robert Matthew: 1991 view (RCAHMS B57226).

90 Norco House, George Street, 1966–70, by Covell, Matthews and Partners; 1986 view. Built as the showpiece Modernist department store of the (now defunct) Northern Co-operative Society, the building was taken over and converted in 1987 by John Lewis; the spired food hall was demolished (RCAHMS A42215).

91 Gray's School of Art, Garthdee, 1964–6, by D. Michael Shewan (RCAHMS B56148).

92   Aberdeen Market and British Home Stores, 1971–4, by Robert Matthew, Johnson-Marshall & Partners; 1990 view. This façade stands on the site of the main façade of Simpson's New Market, with its massive pilasters (RCAHMS B40709).

council began to emphasise rehabilitation of old tenements rather than demolition, and a mixture of private and public building. Emboldened by government reinforcement of consultation and 'listing' in the late 1960s, the city's preservationists, whose work was previously confined to set-piece restorations such as Provost Ross's House and Provost Skene's House (both 1951–2) began to put up more vociferous opposition to major demolition schemes (see also Figures 14, 15, 27, 103, 118, 119, 120 and 124). Such controversies included that surrounding the demolition and re-development of Simpson's New Market in 1971 by Robert Matthew, Johnson-Marshall; or that concerning the demolition of a row of houses at 12–34 Broad Street in 1973 to allow the construction in 1975 of the imposing Town House extension and council chamber (designed by Tom Watson, City Architect between 1970 and 1975) (see Figure 90, and also Figures 22, 23 and 114).

From the 1970s commercial development was more and more constrained and channelled by conservationist pressures into the interstices and edges of the city centre. The schemes of the 1980s, which culminated in Jenkins & Marr's Bon-Accord Centre (1987–90), tended to conceal their

93   Bon-Accord Centre, 1987–90 (Jenkins & Marr): 1989 aerial view during construction (RCAHMS B22547) and 1991 view of Harriet Street car park (RCAHMS B57440). A massive but introverted re-development, filling-in the course of George Street with atrium malls, but largely concealing its full extent behind older street frontages.

bulk behind existing street façades (see Figure 92). Some of these schemes were very large, since in Aberdeen, in contrast to other major cities, the impetus for commercial development had continued throughout the years of economic depression elsewhere: from 1972 onwards, Aberdeen unemployment was around half the national average. For the 1970s and early 1980s were the years when the city and regional economy, following a long period of relative depression, was hit by the 'oil boom' – the most revolutionary regional economic change since the 19th century. Following the sending of probes in 1966 and the discovery of oil in 1969, exotic vessels began to appear in the city, such as the 'Glomar 3' floating oil-drilling rig, which visited Blaikie's Quay in 1971. Oil-industry employment in Aberdeen rose from 2,000 in 1973 to nearly 40,000 in 1985 – by which time 800 firms in Grampian Region were wholly involved in work for the offshore oil and gas industries.

The reason that Aberdeen became the land focus for the oil boom was its geographical potential as a sea and air transport centre. Unsurprisingly, therefore, the most immediate and obvious impact of oil development on the city's built environment was concerned with the enhancement of transport links to the oilfields: namely, a programme of improvements to the harbour, and to Dyce Airport (the hub of helicopter links). By the time the first oil-exploration base was established, by Shell at Torry in 1965,

94 (and opposite)   Aberdeen Harbour and
River Dee, 1996, aerial view from north-east
(RCAHMS C56388).

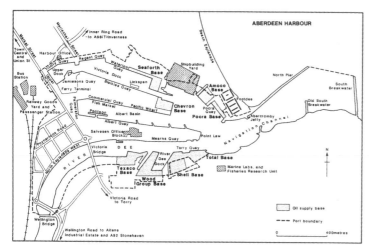

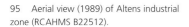

Aberdeen Harbour and River Dee, 1987 layout plan (Northern Times Ltd).

comprehensive harbour modernisation was already underway, led by a reinvigorated Harbour Board and focused on the needs of the fishing industry, which was at that stage still buoyant (but which, by 1980, would begin a steep decline) (see Figure 93). The fishing quays and markets were completely renewed from the late 1960s. As the pace of modernisation accelerated, the docks were converted to 24-hour operation by reinforcement against tidal action and removal of the dock-gates, and a range of offshore supply bases was built around the harbour (especially in Torry and Footdee), both by oil firms for their own operations, and by supply contractors; the oil-supply industry was dominated by North American parent companies. Such bases typically included heavy-duty mobile cranes, mud and cement silo facilities, and oil and water pipeline connections. Other developments included an offshore survival training centre, opened in 1980 on North Esplanade East: as the Piper Alpha disaster of 1988 showed, although oil was a high-technology industry it was also a hazardous one.

At Dyce Airport, the boom in oil traffic led to a thirteen-fold increase in total movements between 1970 and 1983. This prompted the reconstruction of the airport, with a sleek new, beige-clad terminal by John Richards of Robert Matthew, Johnson-Marshall (1978), and the building

95   Aerial view (1989) of Altens industrial zone (RCAHMS B22512).

96   Shell UK Exploration and Production Ltd
headquarters, Altens Farm Road (by McKinnes,
Gardner & Partners, 1975–85); 1991 view
(RCAHMS B56130).

of a new industrial estate at nearby Kirkhill. Away from these transport nodes, planning controls ensured that oil-related commercial and industrial developments were gathered in concentrated zones, above all to the south of the city at Nigg and Altens, where a large industrial estate and office headquarters were built (including the sheer, low slab of Total Oil's office, 1978, by Jenkins & Marr); approximately 1,000 acres of industrial estates in and near the city have been developed since 1975 (see Figures 94 and 95). Overall, despite the shift to a more conservation-orientated planning policy, the built-up area of the city still increased by 15 per cent between 1975 and 1987, and there were large new developments outside the city boundaries, at locations such as Portlethen and Westhill. Within the city, construction of a dual carriageway inner ring road was pushed forward in the 1980s and 1990s (see Figure 96).

The period of the oil boom saw two major reorganisations of local authorities in the area. From 1975 responsibility for the city's built environment was divided between two authorities: City of Aberdeen District Council, with mainly local responsibilities, including housing and local planning, and Grampian Regional Council, which was charged with education, 'structure' planning and other strategic tasks. This division was reversed in 1996, when Aberdeen City Council became a unitary authority once again. The historic Town House has now, once again, the undivided responsibility for steering Aberdeen's civic destiny into the next millennium.

97 Construction of the Inner Ring Road in progress along the Denburn valley in 1992, with the partly demolished 'Triple Kirks' on its left (RCAHMS B70422).

98 Institute of Medical Science, Aberdeen University, built 1994–5 (first phase), by David Murray Associates: one of the most notable works of 1990s contemporary architecture in the city, situated at the summit of the Foresterhill site. This drawing by William Fraser Watt shows a preliminary scheme for the main atrium, flanked by double-height laboratories (David Murray Associates).

Notes

These notes are very selective: their principal purpose is to provide references for direct quotations in the text.

1. J. Rettie, *Aberdeen 50 Years Ago*, 1868, p. 68 (concerning 1615 town council minutes), cited in A. W. Cumming, *A History of Aberdeen Townhouse*, 1975 (thesis, Scott Sutherland School of Architecture), p. 3
2. E. P. D. Torrie, *Historic Aberdeen* (Scottish Burgh Survey), 1997, n. 58
3. A. Anderson, *History of Robert Gordon's Hospital*, 1883, p. 72, cited in D. Murray, *Robert Gordon's Hospital, 1975* (thesis, Scott Sutherland School), p. 34
4. Aberdeen Art Gallery and Museums, *A Tale of Two Burghs*, 1987, p. 47
5. T. Brotherstone and D. J. Withrington (eds), *The City and Its Worlds*, Glasgow, 1996, p. 4
6. G. M. Fraser, *Aberdeen Weekly Journal*, 10 May 1818
7. W. Thom, *The History of Aberdeen*, ii, 1811, p. 188; see also William Kennedy, *Annals of Aberdeen*, i, 1818, p. 351.
8. Aberdeen Press, *Aberdeen Today*, 1907, p. 100
9. T. Donnelly, *The Aberdeen Granite Industry*, 1994, p. 69
10. F. Wyness, *City by the Grey North Sea*, 1966, p. 246
11. J. S. Reid, *Mechanical Aberdeen*, 1990, p. 62; W. W. Watt and E. Watt, *A Century in Aberdeen*, 1941
12. W. Diack, *The Rise and Progress of the Granite Industry in Aberdeen*, ii, 1949
13. *Aberdeen Journal*, 30 June 1888
14. W. Douglas Simpson, *William Kelly*, 1949, see for example pp. 1, 8, 80, 86, 90
15. D. Rorie, *The Book of Aberdeen*, 1939, p. 380
16. *Press and Journal*, 1 September 1937 and 7 March 1964
17. W. Dobson Chapman and Charles F. Riley, *Granite City*, vii, 1952
18. Aberdeen City Council Planning Department files, Director of Planning report 6, December 1977, 'Multi-storey Buildings in Aberdeen'
19. *Press and Journal*, 12 December 1961

PART 2

Architectural and Archaeological Collections

99   King's College Library as
recorded by R.W. Billings c. 1852
(City of Aberdeen Art Gallery and
Museums Collections).

KING's COLLEGE OLD ABERDEEN *as originally built by* BISHOP ELPHINSTON 1500.

100 This view of King's College is from the NMRS Prints and Engravings series. It was drawn by Jamieson and engraved by A. Robertson in 1769 (RCAHMS ABD/31/11).

Introduction

Awide variety of documentary source material exists to help towards an understanding of Aberdeen's development, from architects' design drawings to excavation archives of long-since demolished buildings and early photographs of the cityscape. In common with much of the rest of Scotland, a great deal has been lost, so that the earliest architectural papers to survive date mainly from the early 19th century (the most recent comprise late 20th-century material, the historic documents of the future). Inevitably, the largest volume reflects the building boom of the latter part of the 19th century. The collections described here were created for different reasons: some represent the office papers of Aberdeen architects, some comprise the research papers of eminent local historians, while others have been built up as part of the planning process. Although some of the collections include drawings of the highest quality, others do not. Nonetheless, all have been preserved for the unique information they bear.

Inevitably, all this material is not to be found in one place, but the principal sources are listed below. Many of the nation's collections of architectural and archaeological documentation are centralised in the National Monuments Record of Scotland (NMRS), including the Royal Incorporation of Architects in Scotland (RIAS) Collection and the survey material produced by the Royal Commission on the Ancient and Historical Monuments of Scotland (RCAHMS). Other institutions holding relevant visual material are described under 'Public Collections'. With one exception, these are all located in Scotland. Aberdeen is fortunate in retaining most of its architectural collections within the city, although some important papers have been dispersed, principally Archibald Simpson's drawings.

Three key figures in the study and preservation of Aberdeen's historic buildings are represented here: Dr William Kelly, Dr W. Douglas Simpson and Fenton Wyness. Not only did Kelly and Simpson actively encourage an increased appreciation of the city's architecture, they also played a major rôle in preserving the records of its architects. In doing so, they aimed, as do the curators of these collections, to document what had come before as well as to educate the architects and patrons of the future.

NATIONAL MONUMENTS RECORD OF SCOTLAND

In addition to the collections listed below, the NMRS also holds topographical prints, engravings and drawings, books, sketchbooks, newscuttings, albums and photographs, many of which refer to Aberdeen. The RIAS's collections are deposited with the NMRS, and are denoted below as 'RIAS Collection'. Many of the collections also include material relating to Aberdeenshire.

Aberdeen Archaeological Unit

Since its foundation in 1976, the Aberdeen Archaeological Unit, based within the Art Gallery and Museum, has undertaken numerous excavations of various sites within the City of Aberdeen. The archives from many of the excavations, dating from between 1976 and 1991, are substantial and include site details, notes, drawings, photographs and negatives.

Aerial photography

An extensive collection of aerial photography, both vertical and oblique, is available for the City of Aberdeen, ranging in date from the surveys by the German and British air-forces in the 1940s through to the All Scotland Survey and Royal Commission photographs of the late 1980s and 1990s. The chronological range and variety of the photographs strikingly illustrate the changes and developments of the built environment of the city during these decades.

Alexander Brown Album

A copy of an album compiled by Alexander Brown, an architect partner in the firm of Brown & Watt, which contains press-cuttings and memorabilia relating to buildings designed by Brown in Aberdeen and district in the period 1873–1917. It includes a photographic portrait of the architect and a description of the opening ceremony for Aberdeen Public Library, 1873, which Brown had designed, and for which he was presented with the freedom of the city. Other projects include Old Machar Hospital, opened 1892; extensions to Trinity Hall, completed 1895; the Central Bakery, George Street, opened 1932; and several Free Churches in the Aberdeen area. It also contains a copy of the 1898 Memorandum and Articles of Association of the Aberdeen Society of Architects, and the annual report of the Society for 1899, including a list of members.

Isobel Gordon (b. 1909)

Gordon attended Robert Gordon's College as an art student. She took architectural courses from 1928 to 1933 and was awarded an architecture degree, but did not continue with a post-diploma. This small collection of student drawings comprises competition entries and a measured survey of the South Porch of St Machar's Cathedral. (RIAS Collection)

Historic Photographs

Among the NMRS's early photographs are several 19th-century views of Aberdeen, including a series of George Washington Wilson prints and a set of views transferred from the Records of British Railways, Scottish Record Office.

Hurd Rolland Partnership

A series of drawings recording various stages in a design for the re-development of the centre of Old Aberdeen. The drawings date from 1962 to 1972 and form part of the office papers deposited by this practice. (RIAS Collection)

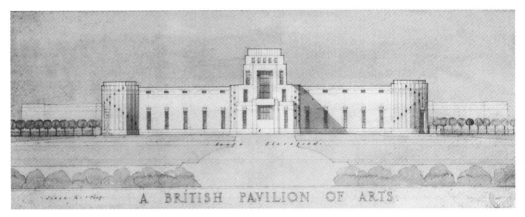

A BRITISH PAVILION OF ARTS

101   Isobel Gordon's design for a 'British Pavilion of Arts'. The drawing dates from the end of her student career (1928–33), and illustrates the quality of draughtmanship achieved under a Beaux-Arts influenced training. Typical of this period is the emphasis on the use of ink washes, something which was to disappear after World War II (RCAHMS C72052).

102   This view from the NMRS Historic Photograph Collection captures the vitality of Aberdeen's Fish Market in 1904 (RCAHMS AB/4047).

103   Provost Skene's House with some of its resident lodgers, c.1890. From the NMRS Historic Photograph Collection (RCAHMS C72486).

104   Robert Hurd & Partners designed the refurbishment of terraced cottages in Wrights and Coopers Place and Grants Place in Old Aberdeen. The design for the landscaped area in between included a memorial to Lady MacRobert and her three sons who were killed in World War II. This perspective is by J. Macdonald, 1963 (Hurd Rolland; RCAHMS D10100)

J. & F. Johnston, Architects

The rise of North Sea oil extraction in the 1970s created opportunities for architects in Aberdeen as the city entered a new phase of development. Several outside practices established offices in the city during this time: J. & F. Johnston of Leith were among them. From 1975 to 1985 the practice carried out a variety of projects in Aberdeen, including the Comex Diving Headquarters. The collection, which was presented to the NMRS in 1994, comprises the surviving office papers. It is not catalogued, although a job-list is available.

Robert William Johnston (c. 1860-1977)

A set of twenty student drawings of buildings in and around Aberdeen, completed in 1905–7 while Johnston was a student at Robert Gordon's College. Includes Aberdeen Tolbooth, interior detailing of Provost Skene's House, surveys of ceilings in an 'old mansion house in Guestrow' and (perhaps the most popular subject in the city for student measured drawing) the Mercat Cross.

F. A. MacDonald & Partners

Several engineering, surveying and architectural firms are represented in this large collection of designs for houses, which graphically illustrates the extent of Aberdeen's late 19th-century housing boom. The firm began as Duncan & Ironside, Civil Engineers, a partnership between Thomas Duncan (1855–1892) and William Dalton Ironside (1866–1915). Ironside was a second generation Aberdeen engineer who succeeded to his father's office shortly before entering into the partnership in 1887. Soon after, the firm amalgamated with that of George James Walker, a land surveyor, to become Walker & Duncan. At this point Duncan had to retire due to ill-health, but Walker & Ironside remained in partnership and went on to become one of the largest engineering and surveying businesses in the north-east. Ironside was principally involved with the engineering branch of the business, and acted as engineer and surveyor to the City of Aberdeen Land Association, where he laid out many of the streets in Aberdeen's west end. Duncan was apprenticed to James Forbes Beattie (1801–77) civil engineer and land surveyor. A small collection of designs for housing in the Aberdeen area (including one design made for Thomas MacLean, Bon-Accord Street, Aberdeen, in 1891), incorporates drawings from Walker & Beattie (founded 1826). Also included in the collection are the drawings of the architect George Coutts (1851–1924), who operated in private practice from 22 John Street, Aberdeen. A special collection of drawings within the F. A. MacDonald Collection is that of the architectural firm Ellis & Wilson (Alexander Ellis, 1836–1917, and Robert G. Wilson, 1844–1931). This was one of the older established practices in Aberdeen. Ellis trained with William Smith before going into sole practice; during that time he designed St Mary's Cathedral, Huntly Street and St Mary's Episcopal Cathedral, Carden Place. For a short time from 1865 Wilson became his assistant, after which he worked for Alexander 'Greek' Thomson in Glasgow before finally returning to Aberdeen in 1869 as Ellis's partner. Ellis & Wilson carried out a great deal of Catholic church work but also worked for the Free Church, United Presbyterian Church and United Free Church (for example, Bon-Accord United Free Church, Rosemount Viaduct). The practice also designed a number of schools, including Walker Road and King Street Schools, and commercial premises such as the Great North of Scotland Railway Offices in Guild Street. Ellis retired in 1894 and Wilson continued in solo practice until 1906, when his son (also R. G. Wilson (1877–1939)) and John Walker joined him, at which point the practice became Wilson & Walker. Wilson retired in 1915 and entered into public service (including a spell on the Corporation's Plans Committee). The Ellis

105 Robert William Johnston's meticulous survey of Aberdeen's Market Cross shows the influence of Sir Robert Rowand Anderson's National Art Survey of Scotland, which encouraged the painstaking study and recording of our country's historic architecture, particularly that of the 15th and 16th centuries (RCAHMS C45198).

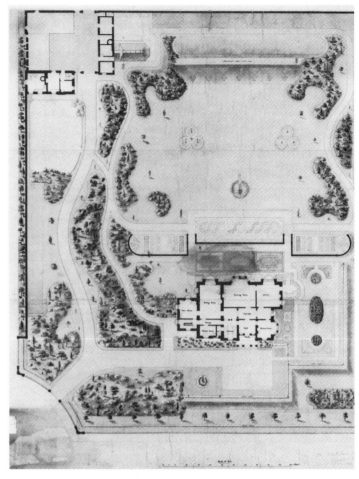

106 An unusually elaborate design for the landscaped setting of a villa, from the F. A. MacDonald & Partners Collection. Dated 1865, it illustrates a scheme for 'Mr Fletcher's House, Carden Place' by Walker & Duncan (RCAHMS C21207).

107 Although this 1890 design for a tenement on the west side of Albyn Grove, Rubislaw is titled 'Plans of Four Houses', the attic floor in fact contained eight dwellings. From the F. A. Macdonald & Partners Collection (RCAHMS ABD/55/4).

108 Design for a mixed commercial and residential development by Matthews & Mackenzie from the F. A. Macdonald & Partners Collection (RCAHMS ABD/149/8).

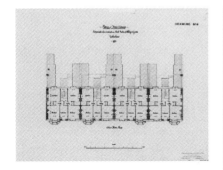

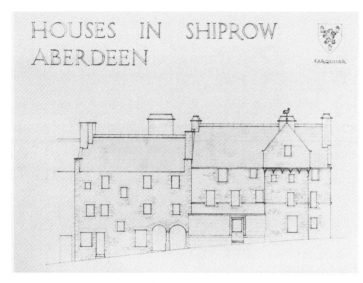

109   A student survey of Shiprow houses by
Edward Meldrum, 1947 (RCAHMS D7485).

& Wilson collection also includes designs
for houses in Queen's Gardens, Aberdeen,
1884, and houses in Menzies Road and
Victoria Road, Torry.

The drawings were ultimately incorporated into the firm of F. A. Macdonald &
Partners, and were acquired by Aberdeen
University Library, who presented them to
the NMRS in 1968.

Edward Meldrum, Architect

Meldrum trained as an architect and worked
in the City Architect's Department. In 1953
he was project architect responsible for the
restoration of Provost Skene's House, which
led to his interest in the preservation of
historic buildings in the north-east. The
collection includes his student drawings
from Aberdeen School of Architecture
(1947 – 8) and measured drawings of Provost
Skene's House, as well as other surveys and
designs for additions and alterations to
buildings in the region.

Peddie & Kinnear, Architects

**Charles George Hood Kinnear (1830–94)
and John Dick Peddie (1824–91) and, from
1881, John More Dick Peddie (1853–1921)**

A set of three pencil sketch designs for
Aberdeen County and Municipal Buildings
(the new Town House), built in 1867–73.
Two of the drawings show the more
elaborate, earlier stages of the design while
the third is inscribed 'original sketch from
which lithograph taken' (RIAS Collection).

James Ritchie (1850–1925)

A remarkable collection of over 400 glass-
plate negatives and photographs of stone
circles, standing stones and other antiquities
taken by James Ritchie, Headmaster of Port
Elphinstone School, Aberdeenshire from
1875 to 1913. Although Ritchie travelled
throughout Scotland, most of the collection
illustrates monuments in Aberdeenshire and
Kincardineshire.

Robert Gordon's Student Drawings Collection

A small collection of drawings dating from
the 1920s and 1930s. The majority are by
James R. Riddell (b. 1907), who studied
architecture from 1924 to 1930; examples
from each session are included. Drawings by
other students include a 1926 reconstruction
drawing by William S. Joss (b. 1904) of the
college as originally built, and a survey of
Bishop Gavin Dunbar's tomb, St Machar's,
by John P. M. Wright (b. 1906) (RIAS
Collection).

110   One of Peddie & Kinnear's elaborate early
designs for Aberdeen's new Town House (see
also figures 60, 134; RCAHMS D5513).

111   Tyrebagger, Dyce, recumbent stone circle,
photographed by James Ritchie in 1902
(RCAHMS AB/2419).

112   The interior of Archibald Simpson's New Market, recorded by RCAHMS in 1965, some years before its eventual demolition (RCAHMS AB/150).

114   The principal apartment of 23 ½ Virginia Street. Although the house was subdivided into flats in the 19th century, this remarkable original decorative scheme, including rococo panels and scalloped shelved buffet niche, survived until the building's demolition (RCAHMS AB/3490).

113   23 ½ Virginia Street, seen in the centre of this view taken in 1973 as part of an RCAHMS survey prior to demolition. This granite-built house, with its rear stair-tower, was built in the mid-18th century (RCAHMS AB/2844).

115   Millbank Mills, Berryden Road, from the south. Recorded in 1983 as part of RCAHMS industrial survey work (RCAHMS A3711).

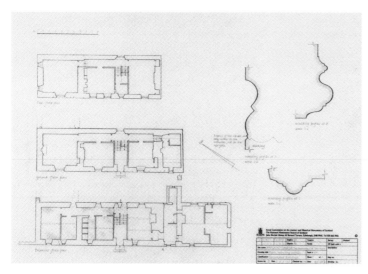

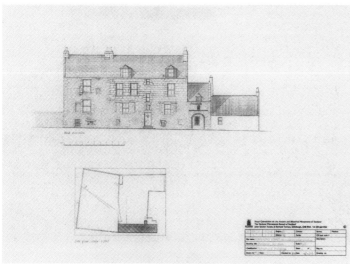

116   Chaplains' Court, Old Aberdeen:
measured drawings prepared by RCAHMS staff
in 1993 (RCAHMS C33297 and C33298).

Royal Commission on the Ancient and Historical Monuments of Scotland (RCAHMS)

The Royal Commission, which was founded in 1908, did not carry out much survey work in Aberdeen until the outbreak of World War II, hence the concentration on the city in the Emergency Survey Album compiled by the Scottish National Buildings Record (SNBR; see below). Following the incorporation of the SNBR into RCAHMS in 1966 and new statutory responsibilities to record listed buildings scheduled for demolition, a new Threatened Buildings Survey was established to undertake more systematic coverage. Simpson's monumental New Market was recorded prior to demolition during this period, as was 23$\frac{1}{2}$ Virginia Street, a charming mid-18th-century town-house with intact interior; unusual 20th-century survivals recorded more recently include the late 1930s Bon Accord Baths, and A. G. R. Mackenzie's Northern Hotel. From 1987, the demand-led Threatened Buildings Survey has been supplemented by the more systematic, topographically-arranged Area Photographic Survey (APS), a rolling programme which includes an element of oblique aerial coverage: the APS surveyed Aberdeen from 1991 to 1992. During the past decade, the specialist RCAHMS Industrial Survey unit has carried out detailed surveys of the Hall Russell Shipyard, Grandholm Works (later Crombie's Woollen Mills) and McKinnon's Spring Gardens Ironworks, in addition to targeted recording of fish-processing and smoke houses.

The results of RCAHMS survey work are held within the collections of the NMRS.

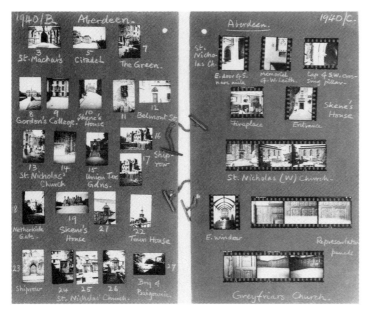

Scottish National Buildings Record

Emergency Survey Album

A rapid photographic survey was undertaken by the SNBR in 1943 with the aim of recording Scotland's architectural heritage in case of wartime destruction. Aberdeen had not been covered by the RCAHMS as part of their Inventory series, and so was a priority for recording. The resulting contact sheets were pasted into makeshift albums. After the incorporation of the SNBR into RCAHMS in 1966, its name was changed to the National Monuments Record of Scotland.

117   Aberdeen's entry in the Scottish National Buildings Record's 'Emergency Survey Album' of 1943 (RCAHMS B41839).

119   The Wallace Tower, or Benholm's Tower, recorded by the SNBR in 1963 before the demolition of the adjacent buildings and the removal of the Tower to Tillydrone (RCAHMS AB/1077).

118   Reconstruction work at Provost Skene's House in 1951, as recorded by the SNBR. (RCAHMS AB/1746).

120   Colin McWilliam's appealing drawing of Provost Ross's House in 1952 for the SNBR is unusual, because the minimal staffing of the Record at that stage normally only permitted photographic surveys (RCAHMS C21177).

Thomas Scott Sutherland (1899–*c.* 1963), Architect

An album of press-cuttings compiled by Sutherland, a flamboyant Aberdeen architect-entrepreneur and city councillor, which records his wide-ranging business and social activities from 1930 to 1960. Controversially, he designed, built and sold houses at a time when this type of property development was unacceptable to the architectural profession. In 1934, he entered the Town Council and two years later became Housing Convener. After the war, he diversified into a range of business activities. During the 1960s, the Scott Sutherland School of Architecture was established in his former house in Garthdee, which he donated and converted for the purpose (RIAS Collection).

Archibald Simpson (1790–1847), Architect

Bound copy of a series of twenty-eight newscuttings, comprising a biography of 'Archibald Simpson, Architect, & His Times' by G. M. Fraser, Librarian at Aberdeen Public Library, and published in the *Aberdeen Weekly Journal* in 1918 (see also Bibliography).

Engraved portrait published in 1849 (one copy in NMRS and one in RIAS) after James Giles.

Dr W. Douglas Simpson (1896–1968)

A small collection of research papers by Simpson, who was Librarian of Aberdeen University Library in 1926–66 and served for a number of years as an RCAHMS Commissioner. Simpson published widely on the architecture, history and archaeology of Scotland. The collection includes correspondence from the 1940s regarding Borthwick Castle and Duirnish Old Church, a collection of proof sheets from MacGibbon and Ross's *Castellated and Domestic Architecture of Scotland* and a

121   These cuttings from Thomas Scott Sutherland's own press-cuttings album illustrate the way in which he captured the city's imagination, as he drove forward the housing programme of the 1930s (RCAHMS C77997 and C77996).

123   John Forbes White's salted paper print of
St Machar's, 1857 (RCAHMS D7403).

122   John Smith's view, 1882, of St Nicholas's Church tower,
which had been designed by his father (RCAHMS D7404).

124   Part of Fenton Wyness's proposal (1948) to secure
Provost Ross's House from the dereliction into which it had
fallen by that date (RCAHMS ABD/40/3).

large collection of photographs. It also includes annotated copies of some of Simpson's books, including RCAHMS *Inventories*.

John Smith (1781–1852), Town's Architect

A collection of papers, dating from 1815 to 1830, which relate to the practical aspects of the architectural practice of this son of a builder. It includes vouchers for subcontracted work, ledgers recording timber used and sold, workmen's rates of pay, cash-books and job-books. Volume viii includes a list of over 200 project drawings.

William Smith (1817–91), Town's Architect, and John Smith Junior (1847–87), Architects

A group of architectural drawings said to be associated with the Smith family of architects, Aberdeen. Includes four presentation perspectives for churches signed by John Smith in 1868, and a sketch view (by John Smith, 1882) of William Smith's tower of St Nicholas's Church. John Smith trained with his father and worked in his office all his professional life, only entering into formal partnership with him *c.* 1879.

John Forbes White (1831–1904), Amateur Photographer

A collection of beautiful early views of Aberdeen taken in 1855–7. The collection comprises waxed paper negatives as well as prints. Subjects include King's College and St Machar's (the figure in the latter is reputed to be the photographer himself). White's chosen technique was somewhat old-fashioned by this time, with its large negatives and long exposure and developing times; but the ethereal effect clearly appealed to him, since he chose it in preference to the clarity offered by the new collodion on glass process. He took no more photographs after 1859, but, after showing his work to the photographer Thomas Annan decades later, he was encouraged to exhibit. Annan printed up three of the negatives, which were displayed at the Glasgow International Exhibition of 1901.

Fenton Wyness (1904–74), Architect

Wyness was an Aberdeen architect in private practice in 1929–64, who specialised in the restoration of historic buildings. He had a prominent rôle in promoting the conservation of historic buildings such as Provost Ross's House and Provost Skene's House. Also a knowledgeable and enthusiastic local historian, he wrote widely on the history and folklore of Aberdeen and the north-east. The collection comprises a series of measured drawings of *c.* 1925 by Wyness and George Watt, for historic buildings such as Crathes Castle, House of Schivas, Fortrose Cathedral and Kinloss Abbey. The collection also includes a number of photographs by George Washington Wilson, which Wyness had inherited from Wilson's son.

DRAWINGS IN ARCHITECTURAL PRACTICES

These records of key practices were surveyed by the Scottish Survey of Architectural Practices (SSAP). The Survey, which was completed in 1996, concentrated on practices established before 1950 which are still active, although some younger practices specialising in conservation work were also included. The existence of an SSAP handlist is noted beside relevant entries; these are available for consultation at the NMRS or by contacting the practices direct.

Hendry & Legge
8 Albert Place, Aberdeen AB2 4RG

Robert A Hendry (d. 1970) and Hugh Legge. *Established 1946*
This practice was begun by Robert Hendry, who went into partnership with Hugh Legge in 1965. All the drawings for the practice survive. Job files for the years 1959–80 relate only to major projects, but those from after 1980 are complete.

Jenkins & Marr
3 Bon Accord Crescent, Aberdeen AB9 1XE

George Gordon Jenkins (1848–1923) and George Marr. *Established 1878*
Throughout the 20th century this practice has contributed major additions to the cityscape. Few early drawings survive, with the exception of the Masonic Temple, Crown Street, 1910 (for which the practice also holds completion photographs). The job files exist from *c.* 1982.

Matthews & Mackenzie

Alexander Marshall Mackenzie (1843–1933) and James Matthews (1820–98).
Established 1842
This practice was hugely successful in Aberdeen in the late 19th century, and its national reputation was assured with the extension of Marischal College in the 1890s. Drawings, photographs and contract books from 1881 survive in the archive of the inheritor of the practice, John Marr Architect, Viewfield House, Old Perth Road, Inverness IV2 3UT.

George Bennett Mitchell & Son
1 West Craibstone Street, Bon Accord Square, Aberdeen AB9 1YJ

George Bennett Mitchell (1865–1941) and George Angus Mitchell (1896–1964).
Established 1904
As well as a broad variety of projects including school and hospital work, major jobs included the Royal Insurance Offices, 208–210 Union Street, Aberdeen, 1910 and re-development work in King's College and Marischal College. Drawings survive from 1901 and job files from 1904, along with a variety of other papers relating to the history of the practice. SSAP handlist available.

Thomson Craig & Donald
4 Carden Terrace, Aberdeen AB1 1US

Ian Thomson, Thom Craig and Robin Donald. *Established 1963*
The records from 1963 survive including job files, a photographic or CAD record of all drawings and a complete job list.

George Watt & Stewart
24 North Silver Street, Aberdeen AB1 1RL

George Watt (1871–1947). *Established 1910*
This practice has specialised from the beginning in school work. Drawings survive for major projects since 1910, while job files survive from 1977.

PUBLIC COLLECTIONS

The collections described here are all available for public consultation, some by appointment. While by no means exhaustive, the principal organisations that hold relevant material are summarised. In some cases, the NMRS has photographically surveyed parts of the collections and this is indicated where appropriate.

Aberdeen Art Gallery
Schoolhill, Aberdeen AB10 1FQ

Architectural Drawings collection
Held in the Science and Maritime History Section, this is a small but significant collection of miscellaneous provenance, which consists primarily of early 19th-century drawings for civic projects. It includes designs for Union Street Viaduct by James Young, 1801, and for Aberdeen Court House by John Smith, 1814. An NMRS photographic survey of the collection was carried out in 1969.

Print Room
The topographical Prints and Engravings Collection contains several examples relating to Aberdeen, principally from the 19th century. The Robert William Billings Collection of twenty-one preparatory drawings for *The Baronial and Ecclesiastical Antiquities of Scotland*, 1852, includes sketches for the two plates of Aberdeen Cathedral and two for King's College, Aberdeen.

Aberdeen Tenement Project
Held in the Science and Maritime History Section, this photographic record of the interior and exterior of selected tenements in Aberdeen was carried out by Charles Morrison of the Bon-Accord Camera Club with the assistance of the Friends of Aberdeen Art Gallery in 1978. The survey focused on surviving original fittings, including hall tiles, ironwork, gas lamps, chimney-pieces and tenant rule boards. An additional survey, also held here, was carried out by the Museum Service.

125   Design for Union Bridge and Union Street by James Young, London, 1801 (City of Aberdeen Art Gallery and Museums Collections, ABMS/6/20).

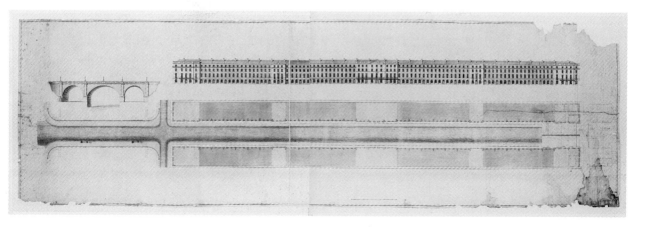

126   St Machar's Cathedral, as drawn by R. W. Billings, c. 1852: view from west and view of nave (City of Aberdeen Art Gallery and Museums Collections).

127   The communal hall of a tenement in Rosemount Viaduct, recorded as part of the Aberdeen Tenement Project, 1978 (City of Aberdeen Art Gallery and Museums Collections).

Aberdeen Central Library
Rosemount Viaduct, Aberdeen AB25 1GW

Aberdeen Maps
This collection of over 200 maps and feuing plans gives a vivid impression of the extent to which the city developed in the 19th century. There are also several important architectural drawings, including some of the few by Archibald Simpson known to survive, such as a 'Plan to illustrate street improvements in Aberdeen', *c.* 1850, and undated designs for Marischal College and the East Parish Church. A selective NMRS photographic survey of the collection was carried out in 1967.

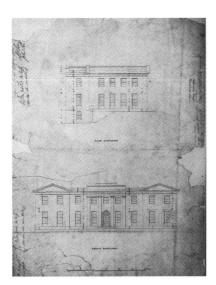

128   Design for Mrs Emslie's Institution, later Aberdeen Girls' High School, by Archibald Simpson, 1837; from the Aberdeen Maps Collection, Central Library, Aberdeen (RCAHMS ABD/99/4).

129   Rockery in Victoria Park, Aberdeen. From the George Washington Wilson Photographic Archive, C1377 (University of Aberdeen, Library Division).

George Washington Wilson
Ten albums of photographic plates pasted on to brown card pages, which were presumably selectively compiled in the photographer's studio. Volume 5, 'Scotland', is labelled 'odd proofs from a series of 25,000 negatives of GB taken between 1866 and 1886'. Although five of the albums have been fire damaged, the prints have been salvaged. (See also 'University of Aberdeen, Queen Mother Library'.)

Aberdeen Architectural Association
A folder of miscellaneous proceedings and drawings recording the early days of the Association, which was founded in 1905. Annual studentships were awarded by the Association; George Irvine, Editor of the Proceedings and Convener of the Committee, explained that these were 'for the purpose of encouraging the preparation of carefully measured drawings from good examples of old building'. A folder for 1909 (vol.1, part 1) includes subjects such as: Robert Gordon's Hospital; Old Houses in Shiprow; Hospital Court; and the Old Grammar School. The plates are by J. Buyers Scott, William Green, Leonard J. Smith, Colin J. Macdonald, A. McD Cruickshank, J. B. Nicol & R. W. Gibbon and S. H. Brown.

Aberdeen Photographic Association
Nine boxes of lantern slides dating from the first years of the Association, which was founded in 1889. The originals are too fragile to be handled but copy prints are available for consultation. Handlists of subjects are available for each box and include 'Historical views of streets', 'Historical structures' and Aberdeen Harbour. In some cases the slides are made from earlier photographic views. They were compiled into a collection for lecturing purposes by David Barker of the Aberdeen Camera Club (formerly the Aberdeen Photographic Association) in the late 1960s prior to deposit with the Library.

130   The old Trades Hall, which stood at the southern end of Shiprow, photographed in the mid-19th century, just before it was swept away by railway development (Aberdeen City Council, Arts & Recreation Department: Aberdeen Photographic Association Collection, Central Library).

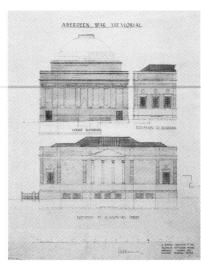

131   Contract drawing for Aberdeen War Memorial by A. Marshall Mackenzie & Son, 1923 (Aberdeen City Archives and John Marr, Architect).

Aberdeen City Archives
Town House, Broad Street, Aberdeen AB10 1AQ

Aberdeen Plans Committee Records
These date from the establishment of a Plans Committee in 1862 to vet proposed building work within the city. From 1947 to 1964 the Committee also dealt with planning permission; those records are held in the Building Control department of the City Council. Full sets of plans, including site plans, only began to be submitted in the 1880s. The number of applications to 1947 totalled 22,000, although only about 8,000 sets of plans survive. The Register gives details of individual applications from 1879 to 1949, while the drawings themselves are indexed in a separate file by address.

Clydesdale Bank Collection
The Bank's papers, which include a number of drawings, record the early history of what was originally the North of Scotland Bank. Included are drawings for the Head Office in 5 Castle Street with designs attributed to Archibald Simpson and David Rhind, *c.* 1839. An NMRS photographic survey was carried out in 1969 when the drawings were still with the Bank. Over half of the 190 drawings recorded have been transferred to the City Archives.

City Architect's Collection
The collection consists of design drawings for various projects executed by the City Architect's Department from the 1890s to 1975, particularly plans for postwar municipal housing. The collection also includes drawings for some Town Council commissions undertaken by private practices, notably a set of contract drawings by Peddie & Kinnear for the County and Municipal Buildings, dating from 1867 to 1870. There are summary lists of projects for which drawings survive.

132   Design for the North of Scotland Bank, 5 Castle Street, Aberdeen, by Archibald Simpson, *c.* 1839. Part of the Clydesdale Bank Collection, Aberdeen City Archives (Aberdeen City Archives; RCAHMS ABD/162/2).

Ashmolean Museum
Oxford OX1 2PH

James Gibbs
Gibbs (1682–1754) spent most of his life in England, where he enjoyed great success, but he was not forgotten by his native city, which made him a burgess in 1739. His principal contribution to Aberdeen was West St Nicholas Church. Gibbs's papers were bequeathed to the Radcliffe Library, Oxford, but have now been split between three institutions. The Bodleian Library in Oxford has part of his book collection, while the Sir John Soane Museum in London has his manuscript Memoir. The Ashmolean Museum holds eight volumes of designs by Gibbs, among them designs for St Nicholas Church, Aberdeen, in Volume III, page 130 (which were produced in 1741, although the church was not completed until 1755), as well as drawings collected by the architect.

The Robert Gordon University
Garthdee Road, Aberdeen AB9 2QB

The University Library has a small amount of material relating to its former students, as well as a few miscellaneous architectural items. These include the drawings of J. B. Nicol (1868–1953); a research file on Archibald Simpson, which contains original drawings of the Chapel of Ease, Woodside (just outside the then Aberdeen burgh boundaries); and miscellaneous prints and engravings of Aberdeen buildings dating from the late 19th century.

Royal Incorporation of Architects in Scotland
15 Rutland Square, Edinburgh EH1 2BE

In addition to the RIAS Drawings Collection, which is deposited within the collections of the NMRS, the RIAS has a collection of portraits of Past Presidents which hang in the Council Room of the Incorporation's headquarters. It includes portraits of two prominent Aberdeen architects: A. G. R. Mackenzie (President 1947–9) and Dr William Kelly (President 1918–20).

Scottish Record Office
West Register House, Charlotte Square, Edinburgh EH1

Major civic projects are represented in the Ministry of Works Collection, including Aberdeen Post Office and Aberdeen Court House. The British Railways Collection also includes Aberdeen material. The Valuation Office Series (Inland Revenue Series, or IRS), which was created under the provisions of the Finance Act of 29 April 1910, includes a set of notebooks that frequently contain block and site plans of properties. Miscellaneous architectural drawings in the topographical run include the Palace Theatre, Walker & Duncan, *c*. 1900; Plan of St Machar's, Ellis & Wilson, 1891; and a plan of houses and sheds at Aberdeen for Sir Archibald Grant Bt, 1753, by John Jeans.

University of Aberdeen
Directorate of Information Systems and Services, Library Division, Department of Special Collections and Archives, King's College, Old Aberdeen AB24 3SW

William Kelly Collection
Dr William Kelly (1861–1944) was a fellow of the Aberdeen Society of Architects and was President of the Scottish Institute of Architects for two years. A Traditionalist architect who was deeply committed to Aberdeen's historic heritage, he worked on the reconstruction of many buildings in the city including the old Royal Infirmary and King's College Chapel. The collection reflects this interest and includes survey drawings of buildings in Old Aberdeen, some drawn on the verso of plates from *The Builder*, as well as designs by Kelly for

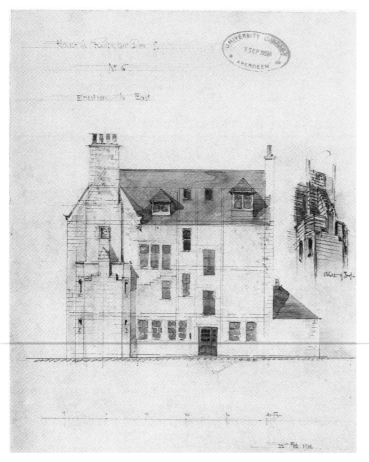

132   Design for the rear elevation of 6 Rubislaw Den, by William Kelly, 1901 (University of Aberdeen, Library Division).

restoration projects such as the Manse, Old Aberdeen. Kelly's office drawings have been incorporated into the Library's Building Plans series. New work includes designs for his own house at 62 Rubislaw Den South. The collection also includes papers relating to Kelly's published analysis of Glenbuchat Castle, *Book of Glenbuchat*.

The Kelly Collection also includes papers relating to two other Aberdeen architects: *William Smith* (1817–91), Town's Architect from 1852. Kelly had been apprenticed to Smith and later went into partnership with him after the death of Smith's son, John Smith, who had been in practice with his father. These papers include correspondence, notebooks and sketchbooks relating to the work of William and John Smith. Projects include Balmoral Castle and the Market Buildings, Aberdeen.

Charles Carmichael (d. 1890). Three sketchbooks, dated 1885–7, which may have been given to William Smith by Carmichael on his departure for Johannesburg in 1889, where his practice, Philip Carmichael & Murray, had a busy office.

W. Douglas Simpson Collection
This large collection of research papers was bequeathed to Aberdeen University Library by Simpson, who was Librarian from 1926 to 1966. It represents his broad interests as an archaeologist and historian of medieval architecture, especially Scottish castles. Included are annotated volumes (many being his own works), pamphlets, nearly 2,000 postcards and photographs and approximately 5,500 3.5-inch lantern slides of mainly Scottish subjects.

Building Plans
This collection derives principally from two sources: the Ministry of Works drawings, which came to the Library in 1937, and William Kelly's survey drawings, which arrived in 1956 (see above). The miscellaneous subjects represented were arranged into broad categories by Douglas Simpson: 'Aberdeen Churches', 'Memorials', 'Old Aberdeen' and 'Public Buildings'. The largest sets of drawings relate to King's College and Marischal College.

University of Aberdeen
Queen Mother Library, Meston Walk, Old Aberdeen AB9 2UE

George Washington Wilson Collection
Collection of approximately 40,000 glass-plate negatives from the working stock of a pioneering Aberdeen photographic printing firm. The views range from the late 1850s to the early 1900s, with a particular emphasis on Aberdeen and the north-east. Film copies and CD-ROM are used for consultation.

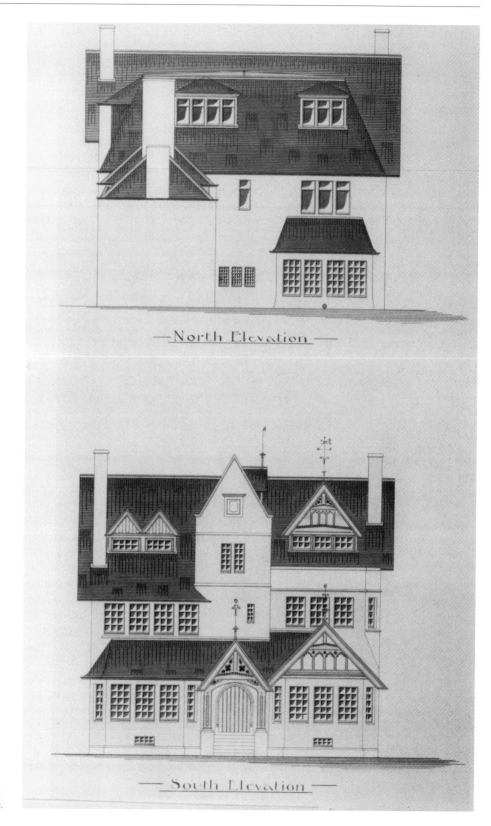

— North Elevation —

— South Elevation —

133 Design for a villa in Queen's Road, Aberdeen by George Coutts, c. 1900. Part of the F. A. MacDonald and Partners Collection (RCAHMS C72462 CN).

Bibliography

This book is based on the following selective group of publications, supplemented by reference to the Historic Scotland List of Buildings of Architectural and Historic Interest. Most 20th-century (and some 19th-century) publications cited here are included in Aberdeen Central Library's extensive local history collections.

ABBREVIATIONS

FSMCOP: Friends of St Machar's Cathedral, Occasional Paper

SSS: Scott Sutherland School of Architecture, Robert Gordon University

134   Town House, 1992 view (RCAHMS B 42721/CN).

GENERAL

Aberdeen Savings Bank, 1967

J. R. Allan (ed.), *The Crombies of Grandholm*, 1960

W. Brogden, *Aberdeen: An Illustrated Architectural Guide*, 1986

W. Brogden (ed.), *The Neo-Classical Town*, 1996

T. Brotherstone and D. J. Withrington (eds), *The City and Its Worlds*, 1996

J. J. Carter and C. A. McLaren, *Crown and Gown*, 1994

V. E. Clark, *The Port of Aberdeen*, 1921

J. Craig, *A Short History of the Royal Aberdeen Hospital for Sick Children*, 1968

J. Cruikshank, *Dyce: Its History and Traditions*, 1934

T. Donnelly, *The Aberdeen Granite Industry*, 1994

R Emerson, *Professors, Patronage and Politics*, 1992

P. B. Enfield, *The Granite Industry of Aberdeen*, 1951

G. M. Fraser, *Aberdeen Street Names*, 1986 (republished)

G. M. Fraser, *Historical Aberdeen* (2 vols), 1904/5

M. Glendinning, R. MacInnes, A. MacKechnie, *A History of Scottish Architecture*, 1996

A. Guthrie, *Aberdeen Football Club*, 1988

I. G. C. Hutchison, *The University and the State*, 1993

A. Keith, *A Thousand Years of Aberdeen*, 1972

A. Keith, *Eminent Aberdonians*, 1984

W. Kennedy, *Annals of Aberdeen*, 1818

I. D. Levack, H. A. F. Dudley (eds), *Aberdeen Royal Infirmary*, 1992

135 4 Golden Square (RCAHMS B55908 CN).

R. W. MacDonald, *A Short History of Torry*, 1995

L. J. Macfarlane and A. G. Short, *The Burgh and Cathedral of Old Aberdeen, 1489–1929*, 1989 (FSMCOP 12)

H. Mackenzie, *The City of Aberdeen*, 1953 (Third Statistical Account)

E. Meldrum, *Aberdeen of Old*, 1987

G. Milne, *Aberdeen*, 1911

D. Morgan, *Footdee*, 1993

D. Omand (ed.), *The Grampian Book*, 1987

J. Rickaby, *Aberdeen – A Complete Record, 1903–1987*, 1987

W. Robbie, *Aberdeen, Its Traditions and History*, 1893

I. Shepherd, *Exploring Scotland's Heritage, Grampian*, 1986 (first edition); *Aberdeen and North-East Scotland*, 1996 (second edition)

A. Smith, *The History and Antiquities of New and Old Aberdeen*, 1882

W. Thom, *History of Aberdeen*, 1811

J. Webster, *The Dons*, 1978/1990

G. Wood, *Torry Past and Present*, 1995

F. Wyness, *Aberdeen, Century of Change*, 1971

F. Wyness, *City by the Grey North Sea*, 1966

CHAPTERS 1 AND 2

Aberdeen Art Gallery and Museums, *A Tale of Two Burghs*, 1987

R. G. Cant, *The Building of St Machar's Cathedral*, 1979 (FSMCOP 4)

I. B. Cowan, *St Machar's Cathedral in the Early Middle Ages*, 1980 (FSMCOP 6)

J. S. Dent, *Building Materials...at Broad Street, Aberdeen* (Scottish Vernacular Buildings Working Group), 1976

W. C. Dickinson (ed.), *Early Records of the Burgh of Aberdeen*, 1957

B. J. Finnie, *History and Development of Old Aberdeen*, 1975 (thesis, SSS)

G. M. Fraser, *The Antiquities of Aberdeen and Neighbourhood*, 1913

J. D. Galbraith, *St Machar's Cathedral: The Celtic Antecedents*, 1982 (FSMCOP 8)

J. Gordon, *Description of Both Towns of Aberdeen*, 1661

J. G. Grant Fleming, *The Story of St Mary's Chapel*, 1935

C. Innes (ed.), *Fasti Aberdonienses*, 1854 *Inventories of Records Illustrating the History of the Burgh of Aberdeen*, 1890

M. Lynch, G. P. Stell and G. Spearman (eds.), *The Scottish Medieval Town*, 1988 (especially essay by H. Booton)

C. McCartney, *The Stained Glass Windows of St Machar's Cathedral*, 1979 (FSMCOP 5)

L. J. Macfarlane, *William Elphinstone and the Kingdom of Scotland*, 1985

L. J. Macfarlane, *St Machar's Cathedral in the Later Middle Ages*, 1973 (FSMCOP 1)

L. J. Macfarlane and A. Short, *The Burgh and Cathedral of Old Aberdeen*, 1989 (FSMCOP 12)

L. J. Macfarlane, *St Machar's Cathedral, Aberdeen, and its Medieval Records*, 1987 (FSMCOP 11)

D. MacNiven, *Merchants and Traders in Early 17th-Century Aberdeen*, 1977 (PhD thesis, University of Aberdeen)

D. McRoberts, *The Heraldic Ceiling of St Machar's Cathedral*, 1974 (FSMCOP 2)

J. Milne, *Topographical, Antiquarian and Historical Papers in the City of Aberdeen*, 1911

A. M. Munro, *The History of Aberdeen Market Cross*, 1910

J. C. Murray (ed.), *Excavations in the Medieval Burgh of Aberdeen 1973–1981*, 1982 (Society of Antiquaries Monograph Series 2)

Record Office, Scotland, *Index to... Registers of Sasines, Sheriffdom of Aberdeen*, vols 1 and 2, 1924/8

E. H. B. Rodger, *Old Aberdeen*, 1902

I. A. G. Shepherd, I. B. M. Ralston, *Early Grampian, a Guide to the Archaeology*, 1979

A. Short, *The Kirkyard of St Machar's Cathedral*, 1982 (FSMCOP 9)

A. T. Simpson and S. Stevenson, *Town Houses and Structures in Medieval Scotland*, 1980

G. G. Simpson, *Aberdeen's Hidden History*, 1974

G. G. Simpson, *Old Aberdeen in the Early Seventeenth Century*, 1975 (FSMCOP 3)

J. Smith (ed.), *Old Aberdeen*, 1991

J. S Smith (ed.), New Light on Medieval Aberdeen, 1985

G. P. Stell, 'Stone buildings with timber foundations', *Proceedings of the Society of Antiquaries of Scotland*, 1984

D. Stevenson, *St Machar's Cathedral and the Reformation 1560–1690*, 1981 (FSMCOP 7)

D. Stevenson, *King's College, Aberdeen, 1560–1641*, 1990

D. Thomson, *The Life and Art of George Jamesone*, 1974

E. P. D. Torrie, 'The Early Urban Site of New Aberdeen', *Northern Scotland*, xii, 1992

E. P. D. Torrie, *Historic Aberdeen* (Scottish Burgh Survey), 1997

K. E. Trail, *Reminiscences of Old Aberdeen*, 2 vols, 1929/32

A. Walker, *The Paroch Kirk of Sanct Nicolas*, 1876

CHAPTER 3

Bicentenary Record of Robert Gordon's Hospital in Aberdeen, 1929

J. J. Carter and J. H. Pittock (eds), *Aberdeen and the Enlightenment*, 1987

G. Evans, *Polite Society in Aberdeen in the 18th century*, n.d.

Filopoliteous, *A Succinct Survey of the Famous City of Aberdeen*, 1685

Foundation, Statutes and Rules of Robert Gordon's Hospital in Aberdeen, 1823

G. Holmes and D. Szechi, *The Age of Oligarchy*, 1993, appendix

D. Murray, *Robert Gordon's Hospital*, 1975 (thesis, SSS)

A. Short, *Old Aberdeen in the Eighteenth Century*, 1985 (FSMCOP 10)

J. Sinclair (ed.), *Statistical Account of Scotland*, vol. 19, 1797

W. Smith, *Diary of an Aberdeen Advocate 1760–1762*, n.d.

CHAPTER 4

'The Archibald Simpson Quarterly Celebrations', *Royal Incorporation of Architects in Scotland Quarterly*, August 1947

The Book of Bon-Accord, 1839

T. Brotherstone and D. J. Withrington (eds), *The City and its Worlds*, 1996 (particularly essay by R MacInnes)

J. J. Carter and J. H. Pittock (eds), *Aberdeen and the Enlightenment*, 1987

F. Farmer, *Early History of Union Street*, 1974 (thesis, SSS)

G. M Fraser, 'Archibald Simpson, Architect', *Aberdeen Weekly Journal*, 5 April 1918 – 11 October 1918

R. Harrison, *Archibald Simpson, Architect of Aberdeen*, 1978

A. Keith, *The North of Scotland Bank*, 1936

J. S. Smith and D. Stevenson, *Aberdeen in the Nineteenth Century*, 1988

Statistical Account, *Aberdeenshire*, 1843

CHAPTER 5

Aberdeen Corporation, *Aberdeen and its First School Board*, 1972

Aberdeen Corporation, *Gas Undertaking 1871–1948*, 1948

Aberdeen Corporation Industrial Development Committee, *Industrial and other Aspects of the City of Aberdeen*, 1909

Aberdeen Corporation Transport Department, *Sixty Years of Progress*, 1938

Aberdeen Press, *Aberdeen To-day*, 1907

R. A. Baxter, *Free St Clement's, Aberdeen*, 1994

Beechgrove Church, Aberdeen: A Record of Fifty Years, 1950

T. Brotherstone and D. J. Withrington (eds), *The City and its Worlds*, 1996

K. D. Buckley, *Trade Unionism in Aberdeen*, 1955

J. R. Coull, *The Sea Fisheries of Scotland*, 1996

A. Courage, *A Brief Survey of Aberdeen*, 1853

A. W. Cumming, *History of Aberdeen Town House*, 1975 (thesis, SSS)

A Descriptive Account of Aberdeen, 1894

W. Diack, *Rise and Progress of the Granite Industry of Aberdeen*, 1949

T. Donnelly, *The Aberdeen Granite Industry*, 1994

A. Gammie, *The Churches of Aberdeen*, 1909

Great North of Scotland Railway Association, *The Joint Station*, 1992

Kingseat Hospital, *Kingseat Hospital 1904–1979*, 1979

D. F. McGuire, *Charles Mitchell*, 1988

M. Mair, *Holburn West Church*, 1993

C. A. Minty, *William Kelly*, 1978 (thesis, SSS)

J. S. Reid, *Mechanical Aberdeen*, 1990

S. Rodger, *In the Slums of Aberdeen*, 1884

J. A. Ross, *Record of Municipal Affairs in Aberdeen*, 1889

W. D. Simpson, *William Kelly*, 1949

J. S. Smith and D. Stevenson (eds), *Aberdeen in the Nineteenth Century*, 1988

A. Symondson, *The Life and Work of Sir Ninian Comper*, 1988

F. Tocher, *Scottish Episcopal Churches in Aberdeen Diocese by Sir John Ninian Comper*, 1979 (thesis, SSS)

H. A. Vallance, *The Great North of Scotland Railway*, 1965/1989

J. J. Waterman, *The Coming of the Railway to Aberdeen in the 1840s*, n.d.

W. H. Watson, *A Marshall Mackenzie*, 1985

W. Watt, *Fifty Years' Progress in Aberdeen*, 1901

W. Watt and E. W. Watt, *A Century in Aberdeen*, 1941

J. M. Wright, *St Margaret's Episcopal Church, Aberdeen*, 1980

136 Marischal College Extension, 1994 view from east (RCAHMS C16708/CN).

CHAPTER 6

Aberdeen Corporation Transport
  Department, *Sixty Years of Progress,* 1958
Aberdeen and District Joint Town Planning
  Committee, *The Aberdeen and District
  Joint Town Planning Scheme,* 1933
Aberdeen Royal Infirmary, *The New
  Infirmary,* 1936
H. Alexander, *Aberdeen and District Joint
  Town Planning Scheme, Papers,* 1934
D. Atherton, *Aul Torry,* 1992
Harbour Commissioners, *Aberdeen
  Harbour,* 1933
R. Hughes and F. Doran, *The People's
  Hospital, the Story of Foresterhill, c.*
  1990
L. Kibblewhite and A. Rigby, *Aberdeen in
  the General Strike,* 1977
D. Rorie, *The Book of Aberdeen,* 1939
T. Scott Sutherland, *Life on One Leg,* 1957
M. Tomson, *Silver Screen in the Silver City,*
  1988

CHAPTER 7

Aberdeen Corporation Transport
  Department, *Seventy-Five Years of
  Progress,* 1974
Aberdeen Royal Hospitals Trust,
  Application for NHS Trust Status, 1991
W. Dobson Chapman and C. F. Riley,
  Granite City, 1952
City of Aberdeen, *Far wis ye fin the Sireen
  blew?,* 1993
City of Aberdeen, *Survey Report/Planning
  Proposals,* 1949
City of Aberdeen District Council, *City of
  Aberdeen,* 1993
City of Aberdeen District Council,
  *Conferral of the Freedom of the City of
  Aberdeen: Councillor Alexander C. Collie
  MBE,* 1995
Corporation of the City of Aberdeen,
  Future Housing Needs of the City, 1971
J. D. Ferguson, *The Story of Aberdeen
  Airport,* 1984
M. Glendinning (ed.), *Scotland Rebuilt, the
  Postwar Vision,* 1997
J. D. Hargreaves and A. Forbes (eds),
  Aberdeen University, 1989
A. H. Harris, M. G. Lloyd and D. A.
  Newlands, *The Impact of Oil on the
  Aberdeen Economy,* 1988
P. Harris, *Aberdeen and the North-East at
  War,* 1987
P. Harris, *Aberdeen Since 1900,* 1988
F. Magee, *The Battling Baillie,* 1978
T. Scott Sutherland, *Life on One Leg,* 1957
J. R. Turner, *Scotland's North Sea Gateway,*
  1986
H. Webber, *City of Aberdeen Official
  Handbook,* 1963

137   Marischal
College Extension,
1994 view of west
façade (RCAHMS
C16709/CN).

Index

Page numbers in bold refer to illustrations or to information in captions

Printed in the UK for The Stationery Office Limited, J26832, C20, 10/97, CCN 020249